Understanding
THE NEW
TECHNOLOGIES
of the Mass Media

Understanding
THE NEW
TECHNOLOGIES
of the Mass Media

GEORGE E. WHITEHOUSE, Ph.D., J.D.

Communications Consultant
The American Consultant's League
Washington, D.C.

PRENTICE-HALL, Englewood Cliffs, New Jersey 07632

Library of Congress Cataloging-in-Publication Data

Whitehouse, George E., (date)
   Understanding the new technologies of the mass media.

   Bibliography: p. 179
   Includes index.
   1. Radio.   2. Television.   3. Videotex systems.
4. Electronic publishing.   5. Mass media.   I. Title.
TK6553.W48 1986   621.38   85-19162
ISBN   0-13-937020-X

Printed in the United States of America

10 9 8 7 6 5 4 3 2 1

ISBN   0-13-937020-X   01

Prentice-Hall International (UK) Limited, *London*
Prentice-Hall of Australia Pty. Limited, *Sydney*
Prentice-Hall Canada Inc., *Toronto*
Prentice-Hall Hispanoamericana, S.A., *Mexico*
Prentice-Hall of India Private Limited, *New Delhi*
Prentice-Hall of Japan, Inc., *Tokyo*
Prentice-Hall of Southeast Asia Pte. Ltd., *Singapore*
Editora Prentice-Hall do Brasil, Ltda., *Rio de Janeiro*
Whitehall Books Limited, *Wellington, New Zealand*

contents

1

the basic principles of electronic media 1

THE COMMUNICATIONS MODEL   *20*

2

the radio broadcast media   *33*

AM (STANDARD BROADCAST) RADIO   *33*

AM STEREO   *41*

3

the television broadcast media   *65*

4

the microwave (terrestrial) media   *101*

MDS (MULTIPOINT DISTRIBUTION SERVICE)
MMDS (MULTICHANNEL MULTIPOINT DISTRIBUTION
SERVICE)   *109*

OFS (OPERATIONAL FIXED SERVICE)   *115*

CARS (CABLE TELEVISION RELAY SERVICE)   *117*

5

the cable media   *121*

MATV (MASTER ANTENNA TELEVISION)   *121*

SMATV (SATELLITE MASTER ANTENNA TELEVISION)   *123*

6

the satellite media   *147*

7

the electronic publishing media   *163*

illustrations

preface

This book is written for those of you who are students or practitioners of any discipline in which you need a general understanding of the workings of the electronic media—especially the "new technologies." It is designed for those of you who have a need to understand the technologies, but have no technological background. It is, therefore, a survey "crash course" in understanding the media technologies for those who do not understand technology.

To be a more competent and competitive practitioner in any communications-related profession, you must understand the new technologies. In order to understand the new technologies, however, you must understand the "old" technologies from which they spring. And to understand any and all media technologies, you must understand the common denominator of all electronic technology: electromagnetic energy. To provide you with a comprehensive understanding, the book starts out with an explanation of what electromagnetic energy is, how it behaves, and how it is managed and harnessed for communications.

The book then proceeds by categorizing the different basic technologies. It is divided by these basic technologies into chapters, each chapter containing the discussions of all homogeneously-related and associated technologies and/or innovations. Further, each individual technology or innovation is contained within a separate section within the chapter. Generally, the first section within each chapter will be a discussion of the basic ("old") medium or technology to provide you with a foundation upon which to understand deviant or innovative developments. This is followed by other sections of shorter discussions of the associated new technologies and innovations. In this way, you should develop not only an understanding of all present technologies (media), but the capability to adapt it to future developed technologies and applications as well. New technologies are not really revolutionary; they are revolutionary from basic principles. These principles do not ordinarily change radically, but remain applicable for years, to both present technologies and those related technologies and innovations developed in the future. What is learned from this book will therefore have diverse and lasting applicability.

This book is written for the student and practitioner who need instant understanding. It is not intended as a scholarly dissertation upon which subsequent scholarly research will be based. Consequently, brevity and simplicity are the key elements to promote this understanding. To this end, scholarly flair, authoritative footnoting, and other distracting literary "bells, lights, and whistles" have been sacrificed for brevity and simplicity. I have taken great editorial license with technical details and explanations for the sake of clarity and conciseness. I offer this as explanation and qualification to both my scholarly and scientific colleagues; however, I make no apology for the means to the end. The contents of the book are based upon about thirty-five years of education, research, training, and professional experience. Its presentational approach is based upon a nearly equal amount of teaching experience. This foundation should be sufficient for the purpose, and the book rests upon its own merits.

acknowledgments

I would like to acknowledge:

The Institute for Communications Law Studies of The Catholic University of America School of Law, Washington, D.C., for its contribution in providing the environment in which to write this book, and for the vote of confidence in adopting it as a primary textbook even prior to its promise of publication.

Harvey L. Zuckman, Director of the Institute, for his personal encouragement, confidence, and moral support throughout this endeavor.

Clark R. Wadlow, of Schnader, Harrison, Segal and Lewis, and Adjunct Professor of The Institute, for his pioneering use of the unpublished text in his classroom.

Commissioner Mimi Weyforth Dawson, Federal Communications Commission, Robert L. Pettit, Legal Assistant to Commissioner Dawson, Erwin G. Krasnow, then General Counsel of the National Association of Broadcasters, for their contributions in the development of my base of confidence.

and the innumerable students, professors, and professional practitioners of my acquaintance in whom I saw the need, and who I hope will benefit.

the basic principles of electronic media

ELECTROMAGNETIC ENERGY

Introduction. It is certainly not necessary to be an electronics engineer in order to participate in electronic communications, any more than one must be an automotive engineer in order to drive a car—even a race car. In fact, too much technical knowledge can often sidetrack and distract one's attention from the operational or other endeavors with which he or she is involved. Often, the best discoveries or innovations are made by those who did not know it was technically not feasible or possible. Therefore, since this book is intended for those readers who are, or will be, involved in other than engineering aspects of communications, it will not burden those readers with unnecessary electronic theory, mathematical formulas, or surreal phenomena.

However, in dealing professionally with others within a sophisticated discipline, the better one understands its substance, the more he or she is able to become more professionally involved—either on a cooperative or competitive basis, or both. A knowledge of the general characteristics and of the language of electronic communication will provide a solid basis upon which to conduct other endeavors, whether they be in communications law, regulation, administration, management, operations, or economics. Fortunately, an adequate level of the necessary knowledge can be acquired without a technical background, if one merely has the patience, ambition, and dedication to endure some mechanical explanation.

Electrical Current Flow.　Recalling some general science knowledge gained back in high school, we remember that all matter on earth is made up of molecules, which in turn consist of atoms, which in turn contain electrons whirling around a nucleus. In some atoms the electrons are tightly bound to their nuclear orbits, while in others the electrons are more loosely bound and can be dislodged from their own nuclear orbit to become "free" to jump from one nucleus to another. When a substance consists of a molecular structure made up of atoms with many "loose" electrons (such as metallic wire) and an electromotive pressure (such as from a battery) is applied to that substance, the loose electrons will flow from one atom to another in the direction in which the pressure pushes them for as long as the pressure is applied. Thus, a flow of electrons, or electrical current flow, is achieved.

AC/DC.　When current flows continuously in one direction, it is called *direct current* (DC). If the current repeatedly and regularly changes direction, such as by alternately reversing the battery pressure (polarity), it is called *alternating current* (AC). It is a phenomenon of alternating current that is the basis of generating electromagnetic energy for use as a communications medium. There are many means available to generate alternating current of different magnitudes and rates, but that is the concern of the engineer or technician. It is enough in understanding electromagnetic energy for the purpose at hand to realize that electrical circuitry can produce electrical currents of incredible rates of alterations.

Radiation.　As current races back and forth in a wire, or any electrical conductor, it releases electromagnetic energy into the surrounding space. Each alternation emits a burst of energy; thus, the faster the rate of alternations, the faster the rate of energy bursts radiated. The alternations of current do not change abruptly from zero to maximum and then abruptly reverse to zero and then to maximum in the opposite direction, but change continually and fluidly (see Fig. 1-1). Therefore, as the current rises and falls in one direction, and then rises and falls in the opposite direction, we can visualize it as traveling back and forth in waves. This alternating flow releases electromagnetic energy proportionately, in proportional waves of radiated energy; thus the term "radio wave."

Power and Frequency.　Each alternation, or cycle, of current flow emits a single wave of electromagnetic energy. The strength or amount of current flow determines the strength (or power) of the emitted wave. The rate or frequency of the alternations of current determines the rate (frequency) of the electromagnetic energy emitted, or the frequency of the radio waves. Thus, a very small alternating current in a conductor will emit a correspondingly weak radio wave. An alternating current of very rapidly changing alternations will emit a correspondingly rapidly alternating radio wave. Note that although the

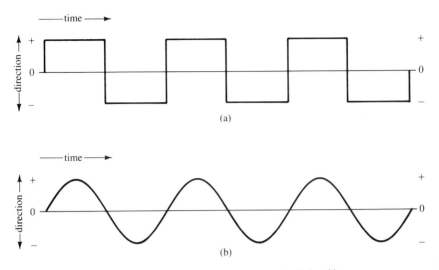

Figure 1-1 Alternating current. (a) Not this; (b) but this.

characteristics of the radio wave are dependent upon the current flow in the conductor, strength (power) and rate of alternations (frequency) are distinctly independent of each other. In other words, a strong wave may be either of high (rapid) frequency or low (slow) frequency, while either may be strong (high power) or weak (low power). There is no interdependence of these characteristics. Note at this point that strength of wave is referred to as *power*, and rate of alternations as *frequency* (see Fig. 1-2).

Frequency Measurement. A single complete alternation of a current or radio wave, from momentary zero through travel in a positive direction through travel in a negative direction back to momentary zero, is one complete cycle. The number of complete cycles that occur within a given period of time (such as one second) is the rate, or frequency, of alternations of the wave. If an electrical current alternates completely once each second, it has a frequency of one cycle per second. It will emit or radiate a radio wave (burst of energy) of the frequency of one cycle per second (see Fig. 1-3). However, after many decades of using this simple and self-explanatory unit of measurement, the powers that be unfortunately decided to complicate the situation by naming this unit of measurement after, and in honor of, the discoverer of radio waves, Heinrich Hertz. Thus, "cycles per second" has become "hertz." Therefore, one cycle per second is now one hertz. (It has been said that these little aggravations are instituted to confuse lay persons and keep competition out of the field.)

Wave Propagation. Radio waves are generated and emitted by electrical current, and possess magnetic qualities; hence the term *electromagnetic*

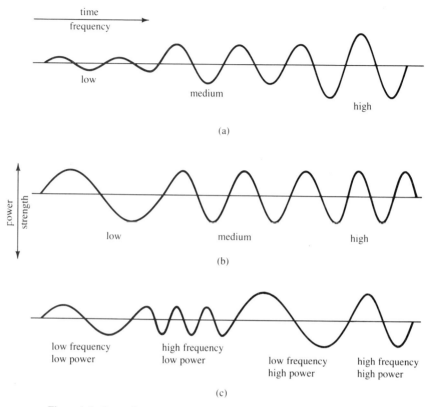

Figure 1-2   Power/frequency representations. (a) Power representation; (b) frequency representation; (c) combined representations.

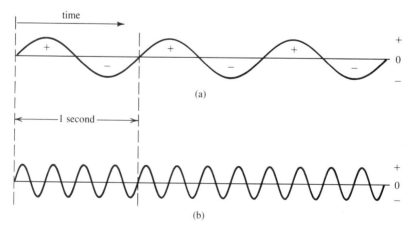

Figure 1-3   Frequency. (a) Frequency = 1 cycle per second (1 cps); (b) frequency = 4 cycles per second (4 cps).

energy. Again we recall a bit of high school general science: Magnetic forces (or poles) of like polarity repel each other, while unlike polarities attract each other. As a single radio wave is emitted, it is immediately followed by a second, and a third, and so on. Each is magnetically identical to the preceding and successive waves, acting like magnets placed beside each other and oriented with the same polarity (see Fig. 1-4). Remember that like charges repel each other; as one magnet is pushed toward the next, that next one is repelled away, repelling or moving before it any that are in its path. Thus, as each radio wave is emitted, it repels or propels the preceding wave before it. As succeeding waves are emitted and travel through space, they are boosted on or propagated by those coming behind, and themselves boost or propagate the ones ahead. This is the phenomenon of *radio wave propagation.*

Speed of Propagation. It must be obvious at this point that the propagation of radio waves through the airspace is dependent only upon the waves themselves; that is, independent from any other medium such as air, water, or any other substance. It is a result of the strength of one radio wave's acting upon another for propulsion. This explains why electromagnetic energy (waves) can

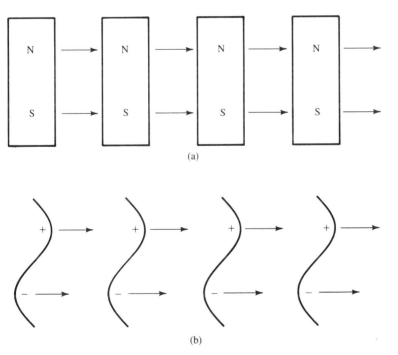

Figure 1-4 Propagation. (a) Magnetic repulsion (magnets); (b) electromagnetic repulsion (electromagnetic waves).

travel through air, space, a vacuum, etc. The speed at which all electromagnetic waves propel themselves is essentially constant and independent of power or frequency. This is the speed of light, or approximately 186,000 miles per *second*. It is, therefore, no wonder that for all practical purposes electronic communication is considered to be instantaneous regardless of earthly distances.

Wavelength.   If a radio wave once emitted were frozen in time and space, it could be measured as to its physical length. The length of that particular wave would be representative of the distance it occupies in space, or the distance it travels during one cycle. Graphically, it would be the measure of one complete cycle of the wave (see Fig. 1-5). Wavelength is therefore a function of frequency. Since electromagnetic energy travels at essentially the same speed (velocity) regardless of its frequency, then either the wavelength or the frequency can be determined mathematically if the other is known. Wavelength is an important characteristic in engineering and antenna (radiator) considerations, and various frequency bands are often referred to by their wavelength equivalents, as measured in meters (the international unit of measurement).

Frequency vs Wavelength.   Although frequency and wavelength can be considered different perceptions of the same thing, it should be noted that they are inversely rather than directly related. That is to say that, because of their inverse relationship, higher frequencies have shorter wavelengths while lower frequencies have longer wavelengths. This is true because more cycles must occur in one second at higher frequencies than at lower frequencies. If more cycles occur within a given time (or space), those cycles must be quicker (shorter). Thus, the higher the frequency, the shorter the wavelength (see Fig.

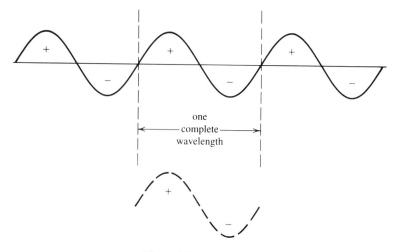

Figure 1-5   Wavelength.

1-6). For illustration, an AM radio station operating at 600 on the dial (600 kilohertz, or 600,000 cycles) would have a wavelength of approximately 500 meters or 1640 feet, while an FM radio station operating at 101 on the dial (101,000 kHz, or 101,000,000 cycles per second) would have a wavelength of approximately 3 meters or 9.75 feet. (An explanation of the metric measurements comes later.)

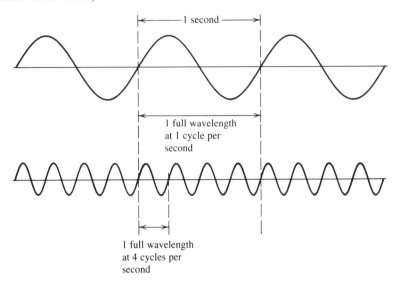

Figure 1-6 Frequency vs wavelength.

Radiators (Antennas).   Any electrical conductor with alternating current within it will emit electromagnetic energy. However, when intended for communications purposes, these conductors are designed for maximum radiating efficiency and are called *antennas*. Antennas radiate energy most effectively when they are exactly the same physical length as the wavelength of the frequency of the energy to be radiated. Expressed otherwise, the antenna should be long enough for the current to flow its exact length during one complete alternation to achieve maximum efficient radiation. However, it would be a bit unwieldly for the AM radio station operating at 600 (kHz) on the dial to erect an antenna over 1600 feet tall! It has been determined that radiation efficiency is satisfactory if the antenna is exactly one-half the wavelength of the frequency, and still adequate at one-fourth wavelength. Thus, antenna size can be made practical at the lower frequencies (longer wavelengths) by designing them at one-half, one-quarter, or even one-eighth of the desired wavelength (see Fig. 1-7).

Summary.   In retrospect, then, it all starts with an electronic generator creating rapidly alternating electrical current through an antenna. The alternating

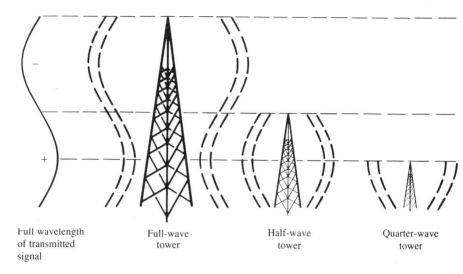

| Full wavelength of transmitted signal | Full-wave tower | Half-wave tower | Quarter-wave tower |

Figure 1-7 Antenna height vs wavelength.

current causes proportionately alternating electromagnetic waves of energy to be radiated into the surrounding space. The power and frequency of the radiated wave are a direct result of the strength and frequency of alternations of the generating current. As the electromagnetic radio waves are emitted, they propagate themselves as long as subsequent waves continue to be emitted; the more powerful each wave is, the farther the waves are propagated (transmitted). Antenna radiation efficiency is maximum when the antenna is exactly the length of a wavelength of the radiated wave, or half-divisions thereof (such as ½, ¼, or ⅛ wavelength). Since wavelength is an inverse representation of frequency, wavelength is longer at the low frequencies and shorter at the high frequencies. Thus, higher frequencies might practically be transmitted from full-wave antennas, while lower frequencies usually must employ a half- or quarter-wave antenna, due to the physical sizes involved. Essentially, a simple antenna radiates in all directions equally; however, they can be made directional, or to radiate more in some directions than others. Once a radio wave is emitted from the antenna, it is propagated at the speed of light (186,000 miles per second) through air, space, or vacuum until absorbed by the environment or lost in space. For all intents and purposes, then, electronic communication is instantaneous.

THE RADIO FREQUENCY SPECTRUM

Introduction.   Electromagnetic energy is the medium for all "wireless" electronic communication. However, electromagnetic energy includes energy that is not used for communication but has other applications. Additionally, although all electromagnetic energy has common characteristics, different frequencies of energy have some different characteristics. Therefore, in order to study electromagnetic energy, to analyze and understand it, it must be visualized, segmented, and labeled. The device used for this purpose is a graphic visualization or chart of all electromagnetic energy by its frequency. This chart is variously called the *electromagnetic frequency spectrum*, the *electromagnetic spectrum*, the *frequency spectrum*, or just the *spectrum*. The overall spectrum can be subdivided into subspectra according to differing characteristics for analysis. Familiarity with the frequency spectrum, at least the radio frequency portion of the spectrum, is absolutely necessary for understanding the nature, the management, and the regulation of electromagnetic energy for communication. Not to understand the frequency spectrum is not to understand the basis of all electronic media communication.

Historical Perspective.   The very early pioneers of radio were cognizant of and familiar with only relatively low-frequency radio waves. The state of the art in those days was primitive, and the technology was physical and mechanical. As a result, radio waves were dealt with in terms of their physical wavelengths and referred to as "long waves," "medium waves," and "short waves," as familiarity with higher frequencies increased. As the technology progressed and higher and higher frequencies were discovered and harnessed, it soon became apparent that actual microscopic wavelengths of these super high frequencies would be immeasurable by standard measures. It became easier to deal with the energy in terms of its frequencies, which became larger and larger instead of smaller and smaller as scientists harnessed higher frequencies. Even at that, the numbers became so large that metric terms and then powers of ten had to be employed.

The Electromagnetic Spectrum.   As previously explained, electromagnetic energy is measured by its frequency (cycles per second, or hertz). Thus, the lowest frequency is one hertz and the highest is infinite, and all electromagnetic energy falls somewhere in between. However, not all of this energy is useful for communication purposes. Only those frequencies which have desirable propagation characteristics and manageable wavelengths are suitable for communications. This group of frequencies is called the *radio frequency spectrum*, which includes all electromagnetic energy that is radiated for communications purposes, including: radio, television, radar, microwave, etc. The frequencies below and above the radio frequency spectrum are not adequately manageable for normal communication purposes because of their propagation characteristics, wavelengths, physical effects, or otherwise. Thus, for all practical purposes, those frequencies between 30,000 and 300,000,000,000 hertz comprise the usable radio communications spectrum. Those below are considered electrical power and audio (aural) frequencies, while those above are physiological frequencies that affect the human body (see Fig. 1-8).

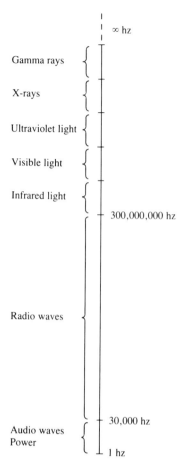

Figure 1-8 Electromagnetic spectrum.

Metric Measurement.   At this point it is obvious that we must deal with tremendously unwieldly numbers. Frequencies in the millions and trillions are typical in many communication applications. (A satellite system typically operates in the 12,000,000,000 hertz range.) Such numbers are impossible to use on charts and graphs, not to mention the problems in engineering mathematical calculations. To relieve this situation the metric system of measurement is employed. Very simply stated, it eliminates the need to express groups of zeros (or decimal places) by assigning short metric names to substitute for them. Thus, a thousand (three zeros) becomes a *kilo*, a million (six zeros) becomes a *mega*, a billion (nine zeros) becomes a *giga*, and a trillion (twelve zeros) becomes a *terra* (see Fig. 1-9). Armed with this shorthand method of dealing with large frequencies, we can manage an analysis of the radio frequency segment of the electromagnetic spectrum.

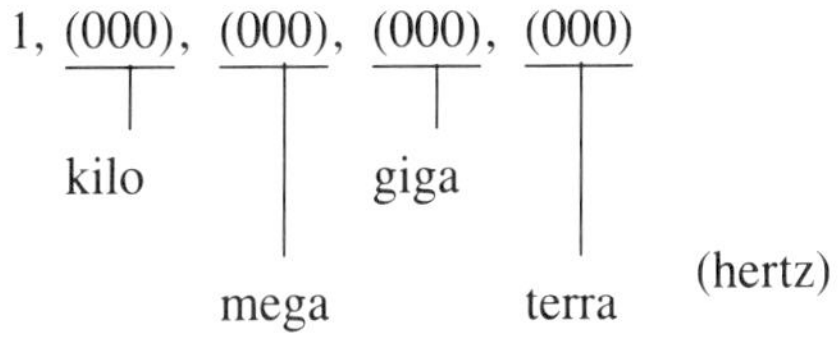

$$1, \underbrace{(000),}_{\text{kilo}} \underbrace{(000),}_{\text{mega}} \underbrace{(000),}_{\text{giga}} \underbrace{(000)}_{\text{terra}}$$

(hertz)

or

$$1,000,000,000,000 \text{ Hz} = 1,000,000,000 \text{ kHz} =$$
$$1,000,000 \text{ mHz} = 1,000 \text{ gHz} = 1 \text{ thz}$$

or

1,000 Hz = 1 kHz (kilohertz)
1,000,000 Hz = 1 mHz (megahertz)
1,000,000,000 Hz = gHz (gigahertz)
1,000,000,000,000 Hz = 1 thz (terrahertz)

Figure 1-9 Metric measurements.

Radio Frequency Spectrum.   The lower practical limit of the electromagnetic spectrum for communication purposes is about 30 kHz (30 kilohertz, or 30,000 hertz). The upper practical limit is about 300 gHz (300 gigahertz, or 300,000,000,000 hertz). Therefore, all frequencies within the bounds of these outer limits are considered the radio frequency spectrum. These are the frequencies that are used for all radiated communication, including radio broadcasting, television, satellite communications, radar, amateur radio, cellular radio, private radio, citizens band radio, and the like—virtually all of the wireless communication media in normal service today. The frequencies within this wide range, however, have some differing behavioral characteristics which make different subgroups of them more or less desirable for different applications. The Federal Communications Commission (FCC), whose job it is to manage the spectrum assignments, has divided the radio spectrum into bands of frequencies for better study and management (see Fig. 1-10).

Frequency Bands.   The radio frequency spectrum is divided into seven bands. The dividing points were selected because of their ease in metric mathematical calculations. Each band is designated as LF (low frequency), MF (medium frequency), HF (high frequency), VHF (very high frequency), UHF (ultrahigh frequency), SHF (superhigh frequency), and EHF (extremely high frequency). Although for study purposes abrupt divisions are made between the bands, the physical and electrical characteristics of frequencies between adjacent bands are not abruptly different, but change gradually from band to band. In

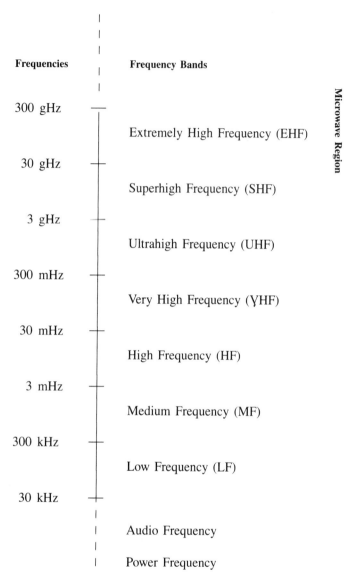

Figure 1-10 Radio frequency spectrum.

other words, characteristics of one band of frequencies overlap into the adjacent band, and there are no sharply distinguished differences between adjacent bands. Characteristics change gradually as frequency changes gradually.

Wavelength.   Since wavelength is an inverse physical characteristic of frequency, as frequency increases, wavelength decreases proportionately. At the lower limit of the LF band (30 kHz), wavelength of the radio wave is roughly 40,000 feet long. At the upper limit of the EHF band (300 gHz), wavelength is roughly .04 inch long. Recalling the previous discussion of the relationship between wavelength and antenna size, this familiarity becomes important in later understanding the use of different types of antennas such as radio towers, TV masts, microwave dishes, etc. Incidentally, the EHF and SHF bands are often referred to as microwave bands (frequencies) because of the almost microscopic wavelengths at these frequencies (see Fig. 1-11).

Propagation. With reference to Fig. 1-11, after a radio wave has been radiated into the surrounding space, it exhibits propagation characteristics

Frequency	Approx. Wavelength	Frequency Band	Propagation Characteristics	Communications Application
300 gHz	.04 in.			
		EHF (extremely high frequency)	Line of sight (focused beam)	Research Satellites
30 gHz	.4 in.			
		SHF (superhigh frequency)	Line of sight (focused beam)	Relays Satellites
3 gHz	4 in.			
		UHF (ultrahigh frequency)	Line of sight (direct wave)	TV
300 mHz	4 ft.			
		VHF (very high frequency)	Line of sight (direct wave)	TV FM radio
30 mHz	40 ft.			
		HF (high frequency)	Ground wave and sky wave (medium range)	Shortwave radio
3 mHz	400 ft.			
		MF (medium frequency)	Ground wave and sky wave (long range)	AM radio
300 kHz	4000 ft.			
		LF (low frequency)	Ground wave (very long range)	Aeronautical Maritime
30 kHz	40,000 ft.			

Microwave Region spans from 300 gHz through 3 gHz.

Figure 1-11 The radio frequency spectrum chart.

associated with its wavelength (or frequency). Generally speaking, the longer the wavelength (or lower the frequency), the more the wave tends to travel along and through the surface of the earth, following the curvature of the earth. The shorter the wavelength (or higher the frequency), the more the wave tends to travel in a straight line, impervious to the curvature of the earth or its topography. Looking at the radio frequency spectrum as a whole, we can generalize that the very low frequencies can move along the surface of the earth over great distances, that superhigh frequencies travel straight beyond the horizon into space, and that the frequencies in between have characteristics of both, correlative to their position in the spectrum according to frequency. This generalization holds true to frequencies compared within a designated band as a microcosm of the overall radio spectrum, but naturally to a lesser degree. In referring to the propagation characteristics of electromagnetic energy, the terms *wavelength* and *frequency* are often used interchangeably to refer to the radio wave.

Ground Waves.   The lower frequencies (LF, MF, HF) in the radio spectrum, since they travel along and through the ground, are referred to as *ground waves* (see Fig. 1-11). These ground waves tend to hug the earth, penetrating mountains, buildings, and forests. They follow the curvature of the earth and travel until finally totally absorbed. The distance a ground wave will travel before being absorbed depends upon how low its frequency is, how much power is in the radiated wave, and the conductivity (mineral/moisture content) of the ground over which the wave is traveling. Arid regions absorb a ground wave sooner than fertile or water surfaces. The long wavelengths of these low frequencies make them stable and predictable. These lower frequencies are therefore well suited to long-range reliable and stable communication functions. A drawback to these frequencies, however, is the massive size of the transmission equipment required, especially the antennas. Recall that the antenna's physical size is determined by wavelength, and wavelengths at these frequencies measure hundreds or thousands of feet long. The preceding characteristics are applicable in relative degree to the frequency position in the spectrum: the lower the frequency, the more pronounced the characteristics (see Fig. 1-12).

Direct Waves.   The higher frequencies (VHF, UHF, SHF, EHF) in the radio spectrum, since they tend to travel in straight lines (line of sight), are

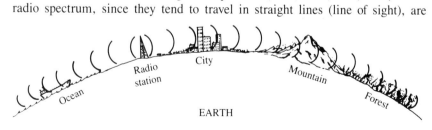

Figure 1-12 Ground wave characteristics.

known as *direct waves* (see Fig. 1-11). The highest direct waves have a tendency to behave similarly to light. Traveling in a straight line directly from one point to another, direct waves are at least partially absorbed by obstacles encountered in their paths such as buildings, trees, hills, mountains, and the like; and may be totally blocked by a mountain, skyscraper, or similar obstacle. The higher of these frequencies may be deflected or reflected off surfaces encountered. As the wave travels, it is impervious to the curvature of the earth, and travels a straight line beyond the horizon into space. Therefore, the direct wave cannot be relied on for communications beyond the horizon, which is roughly 35 to 40 miles away from any given point in any direction. The horizon can be extended somewhat by elevating the source of the signal and/or the receiving site (the higher you are, the farther you can see). Thus, the nature of short wavelengths (high frequencies) is rather unstable and unpredictable, but reliable for communications in a direct line-of-sight application (such as to a satellite). Since communication is limited to the horizon, antennas often must be mounted on extremely tall towers or mountain tops to increase that line-of-sight distance (the horizon) a little farther. Also, since the extremely high frequencies behave similarly to light and have a very short wavelength, a parabolic "dish" antenna is often used to focus the radio waves into a concentrated beam for more effective point-to-point communications (see Fig. 1-13).

The Ionosphere. Much radiated energy, by accident or design, is emitted skyward. Some of this energy is, of course, absorbed by the atmosphere. The radio waves that are not totally absorbed, however, travel into space until they encounter the ionosphere. This is a layer of ionized gas enveloping the earth at a distance of approximately 50 to 250 miles above the earth's surface. Since the ionosphere is created by cosmic rays from the sun bombarding the atmosphere, this distance varies from day to night and season to season.

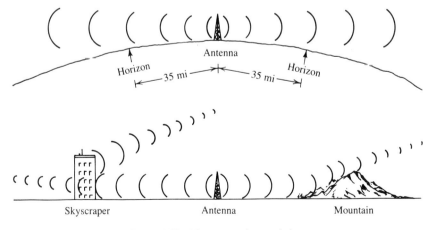

Figure 1-13 Direct wave characteristics.

Different frequencies reaching the ionosphere are affected differently by it. Generally speaking, lower and medium frequencies are absorbed, higher frequencies are reflected back to earth, the ultrahigh frequencies penetrate into space in a refracted trajectory, while the superhigh and extremely high frequencies penetrate into space without much of any effect from the ionosphere. Since low-frequency energy is absorbed by the ionosphere, low frequencies are not suited for space communication, and neither are low-frequency ground wave communications much affected by the ionosphere. The frequencies at the highest end of the spectrum are well suited for space communications, and the ionosphere has no appreciable effect on those frequencies being used for direct wave earthly communications. It is the middle frequencies which are reflected back to earth that affect terrestrial (surface) communications. These reflected waves are referred to as *sky waves* or *skip waves* (see Fig. 1-14).

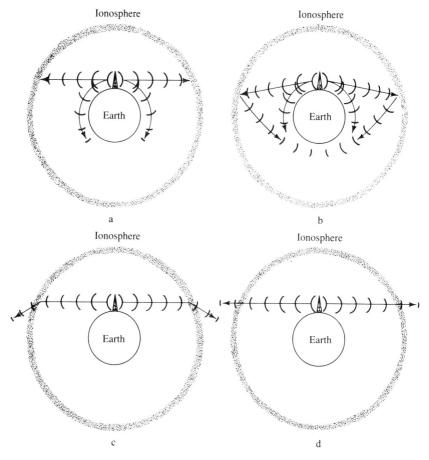

Figure 1-14 Ionospheric effects. (a) LF and MF bands; (b) HF band; (c) VHF and UHF band; (c) SHF and EHF band.

Sky Wave. Sky (or skip) waves are primarily medium and high frequencies which are reflected back to earth by the ionosphere. Because the ionosphere expands and contracts from day to night, medium frequencies are generally absorbed during the day but are reflected back to earth at night at a wide "skip" distance angle, providing for a very long-range nighttime service. High frequencies are reflected back both day and night, providing day and night long-range service. In fact, these waves reflected back to earth may, if powerful enough, reflect off the earth back to the ionosphere, where they are reflected back a second time, and perhaps a third and fourth. This "skipping" wave can conceivably traverse the entire circumference of the earth, providing long-range service, indeed! It is no wonder that international and worldwide communications employ the HF frequencies (the so-called "short wave" frequencies). It must be remembered, though, that these skip waves create skip zones where no signal is received. Since the ionosphere continuously and gradually expands and contracts with the sunlight, constantly changing the angle of reflection, these skip waves and skip zones constantly change during a 24-hour period. However, since the cycles are predictable, so are skip wave communications services (see Fig. 1-15).

Interference. Radio waves can be distorted or interfered with by other undesirable electromagnetic disturbances. These are of two general types: natural and man-made. Natural interference can come from any natural phenomenon which can generate electromagnetic energy of spurious and random frequencies, some of which are the same frequency as the radio wave. These sources include lightning, sun spots, aurora borealis (the "northern lights"), and similar electrical phenomena. Man-made interference can come from any man-made device which emits undesirable and spurious electromagnetic energy of random frequencies, which include those of the radio wave. These sources typically are anything that generate electrical sparks, such as motors, arc welders, lamps, fluorescent lights, neon lights, and even automobile spark plugs. Additionally, one man-made radio wave can distort another man-made radio wave of the same frequency through direct or reflected interference.

Antennas. To reiterate and expand on a previous discussion of antennas, they radiate at maximum efficiency when they are exactly the equivalent of one wavelength long of the frequency being radiated. However, wavelengths at the lower end of the spectrum (ground waves) can be hundreds and thousands of feet long, making it highly impractical to erect such long or tall antennas. This problem is resolved by sacrificing some antenna efficiency by using half-wave, quarter-, or even eighth-wave antennas. Even so, some antennas still must be several hundred feet long. Antennas also must be good electrical conductors. Because of these two factors, ground wave antennas (for frequencies in the LF, MF, and HF bands) nearly always consist of a steel tower (for conductivity and strength) rising to the height of one-half or one-quarter wavelength. The entire tower acts as the radiator, or antenna.

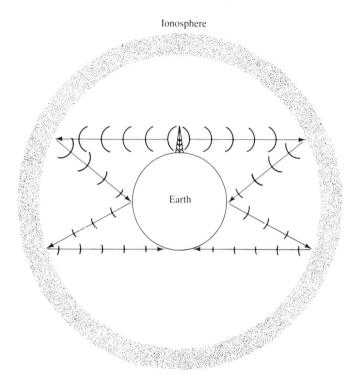

Figure 1-15   HF/MF sky wave (skip wave).

Wavelengths in the direct wave VHF and UHF bands range from about 40 feet to 4 inches. Direct wave antennas can therefore be full-wave or at least half-wave metallic masts. However, to extend the line-of-sight range of these frequencies, the antenna mast is usually placed on top of a tall supporting tower. In this case, the tower is used for an elevation platform, and only the mast on top radiates. (Although an antenna site might be shared by mounting a UHF mast antenna on top of an MF tower antenna.)

In the microwave region of the SHF and EHF bands, wavelengths may be as small as .04 inch. Since these tiny wavelengths are difficult to physically handle, are rather unstable, and behave much like light, their special radiators are often mounted within a parabolic reflector (or "dish") to focus the radio waves into a concentrated beam for maximum radiation efficiency of point-to-point communication. They can then be aimed to "shoot" their waves to a particular location that is within line of sight (see Fig. 1-16).

Summary.   The radio frequency spectrum consists of all frequencies of electromagnetic energy that are practical for harnessing for radiated communication purposes. This spectrum therefore excludes those frequencies below, which

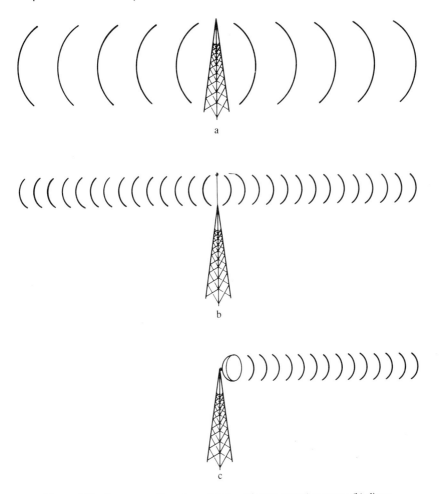

Figure 1-16 Antenna configurations. (a) Ground wave (tower) antenna; (b) direct wave (mast) antenna; (c) microwave (focused parabolic dish) antenna.

are impractical for radiation, and those above, which have a physiological effect on the human body. This radio spectrum extends from 30 kHz to 300 gHz, and is subdivided into seven bands: LF, MF, HF, VHF, UHF, SHF, and EHF. Because of the large numerical values involved, using metric designations facilitates managing these figures. Different frequencies have different behavioral characteristics, depending upon their wavelength. Longer wavelengths travel at the surface of the earth (ground waves), following the curvature of the earth, penetrate obstacles, are stable and highly predictable, and are therefore utilized for reliable long-range terrestrial communications services.

Medium wavelengths have both a ground wave and a sky wave. The characteristics of the ground wave are not as pronounced as with lower frequencies, but exhibit some of the same qualities to a lesser extent. Some of its energy which travels skyward is reflected back to earth from the ionosphere as sky waves, or "skip waves." These make the medium wavelengths excellent for extremely long-range service; however, the sky wave varies continuously but predictably, making this long-range service periodic but reliable. The ground wave component is very stable and reliable for medium-range constant terrestrial communication service.

Short wavelengths tend to travel in direct line-of-sight paths, tending to be absorbed or reflected by obstacles encountered. Since they do not follow the curvature of the earth, they travel to the horizon and straight beyond into space. Since the horizon is approximately 35 to 40 miles away, ground communication is generally limited to this short distance. These radio waves penetrate the ionosphere. Short wavelengths are therefore rather unreliable and unpredictable, but are excellent for use in line-of-sight short-range service and for space communications.

Translating wavelength into frequency (the more popular reference), we can generalize that the lower frequencies provide constant long-range service, the middle frequencies provide constant medium-range service and extremely long-range skip wave service, while the highest frequencies provide short range and space communications service (refer to Fig. 1-11).

THE COMMUNICATIONS MODEL

Introduction.   Regardless of whether electromagnetic energy is used for radio, television, data, or any other form of communication, there is a common basic model or structure for all such communications systems. Just as motor vehicles are used for transportation of all kinds, all vehicles have a commonality of similarly interconnected parts that are essential. Regardless of whether a motor vehicle is designed as a sedan, race car, pickup truck, station wagon, or 18-wheeler, all have common elements. Each must have an engine, chassis, wheels, drive train, and body; each of these elements must be connected similarly to work properly. Therefore, if one can understand the basic model of motor vehicles, he or she generally understands the operation of all motor vehicles. So it is with radio communication: An understanding of the basic model and its essential parts provides an understanding of any application or adaptation of that model to any form of communication system. After all, radio communication, like motor vehicles, is merely used as a conveyance—with information or intelligence as its cargo.

Overview.   All forms of radio communication involve the generation, transmission, and reception of intelligible radio waves from one place to another. The distinctive difference in types of communications systems are the frequencies employed, the kind of intelligence conveyed, and whether it is transmitted for general public reception or point-to-point communication. However, a basic system model is applicable equally to all systems. The generation of the intelligible radio wave is accomplished by a radio transmitter. Transmission concerns itself with the propagation of the radio wave from the transmitting antenna through surrounding space to receiving antennas. Reception is the function of a radio receiver to detect the radio wave and to display its intelligence. The overall model, therefore, consists of a transmitter, propagated signal (intelligible waveform), and one or more receivers. (Note that from this point on, the terms *radio wave* and *signal* will be used synonymously. See Fig. 1-17.)

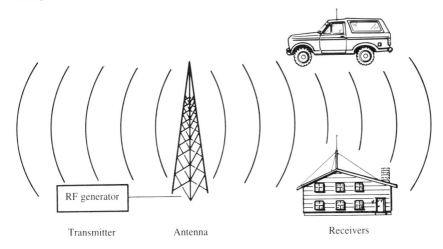

| | | |
| Transmitter | Antenna | Receivers |

Figure 1-17 Basic communication system.

Qualification.   Since this book is written for those who would use this knowledge as a means to professional ends (as administrators, regulators, lawyers, communicators, managers, programmers, etc.) rather than technical ends (as engineers or technicians), it will not be concerned with the intricacies of electronic equipment or electronic processes. But, since an understanding of the overall communication system is the concern, familiarity with the basic processes and requirements of generating, transmitting, and receiving a signal is necessary. In other words, although we won't belabor the details, we must become acquainted with the system processes and the general hardware that provides those processes.

Generation of the Signal

Overview.   The radiated signal is created and formed by a complex of electronic circuitry known as the *radio frequency (RF) transmitter*. This can be a single unit smaller than a hand-held walkie-talkie, or a complex of units housed in separate buildings over acres of ground that in combination form a single transmitter. The size of a transmitter is dependent upon many factors: power, frequency, type of intelligence transmitted, and other factors. Generally speaking, size is directly related to power, but inversely related to frequency. Usually, the more powerful the transmitter is, the bigger it must be. This is true because the circuitry needs large electrical components to dissipate the heat generated by the large amounts of electrical current involved. The transmitter requires a large power supply to produce that current, and often with very high power circuits special liquid cooling systems must be employed. Size is often dictated by the operating frequency, as well. Higher frequencies have shorter wavelengths, which require smaller electrical components and circuits, while the longer wavelengths of lower frequencies require larger components and circuits. Thus, a low-frequency high-powered transmitter can be a tremendously huge facility, while extremely high-frequency and very low-powered transmitters might be as tiny as an olive.

The Transmitter.   The function of any communication transmitter is to generate a radio frequency (RF) wave, to impress upon it (or inject into it, as you prefer) some form of intelligence, and to amplify that intelligible RF wave (signal) to a power adequate to radiate it from the antenna with sufficient propagation to travel as far as desired. Any transmitter, therefore, has basically three essential functions or stages: an RF generator, an intelligence mixer (modulator), and a power amplifier (see Fig. 1-18).

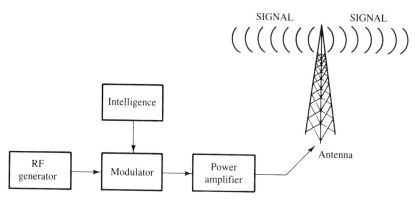

Figure 1-18   Basic transmitter system.

The Carrier Wave.   The RF generator electronically produces the electromagnetic energy of the desired operating frequency. This frequency is commonly called the *carrier wave*, because of its sole function to carry some form of intelligence from one place to another. As we have seen, RF energy propagates through the atmosphere and space. The forms of intelligence which we use (sound, pictures, data, etc.) do not. They must be carried wherever we want them to go. Thus, they must somehow be piggybacked on the carrier wave.

The Intelligence.   The forms of intelligence to be conveyed are generally sound, pictures, or data. Since these are to be carried on an electronic carrier wave, they must be converted first into electronic form in order to be mixed with the carrier. Sound is generally converted by microphone into electrical form (audio frequencies). Since audio frequencies are below the lowest radio frequencies on the spectrum, they do not propagate. Pictures are generally converted by television camera into electronic form (electrical pulses and variations), which also cannot propagate. Data is transformed by a number of devices (such as computers) into electrical form (pulses of energy), which also does not propagate. Once any of this intelligence is in electronic (or electrical) form, it can be mixed with the electronic carrier wave to travel with it. This process of mixing the intelligence with the carrier wave is called *modulation* (see Fig. 1-19).

Modulation.   Modulation, or the mixing of electronic intelligence with an RF carrier, is the function of the modulator stage of the transmitter. To be very simplistic, as the carrier frequency travels through the modulator, the modulator

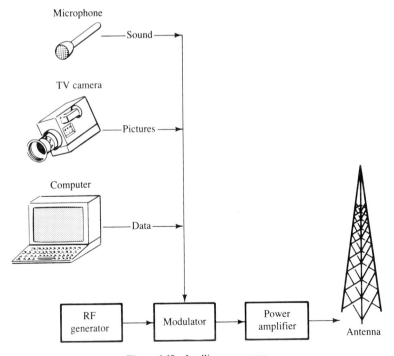

Figure 1-19 Intelligence sources.

uses the intelligence frequency (or pulsing) like a valve to vary the carrier accordingly. If the modulator is designed to vary the amplitude or strength (power) of the carrier, it is called *amplitude modulation*. If the modulator is designed to vary the frequency of the carrier, it is called *frequency modulation*. In either case, however, the amplitude or the frequency of the carrier will vary exactly in accordance with the variations of the intelligence. The carrier then proceeds with its own characteristics intact, but containing the exact variations (frequencies or pulses) in replica of the intelligence. The carrier has been modulated by the intelligence information, which the receiver will later detect and convert back into the original intelligence form (see Fig. 1-20).

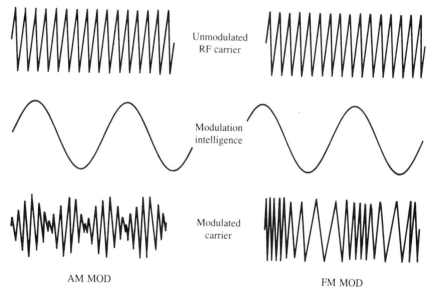

Unmodulated RF carrier

Modulation intelligence

Modulated carrier

AM MOD

FM MOD

Figure 1-20   Modulation.

AM/FM.   Generally, any type of modulation can be used with any carrier frequency. When the FCC requires a specific kind of modulation to be used within a particular service allocation, such as amplitude modulation for the standard broadcast band (AM radio), it is done purely for arbitrary, regulatory, or performance purposes rather than because of technological necessity. To illustrate, when radio broadcasting began, it was assigned to the lower end of the spectrum (MF band), because the upper regions of the spectrum had not been harnessed for use, yet; AM modulation was required because no other form of usable modulation existed at the time. Many years later, when a second broadcast radio service was established, it was assigned to the much higher VHF band and designated for FM modulation only to provide for better music channels. Frequency modulation is not subject to electrical interference to the degree that amplitude modulation is. Television, however, employs both types of modulation within its signal; AM for picture information and FM for sound information.

The Sidebands.   When a carrier wave is pure, before it is modulated, it consists of energy of a single frequency. After it is modulated, however, it consists of itself plus the frequencies of the modulating energy. Recall that the modulating variations caused the carrier to both increase and decrease; thus, the frequency of the modulating energy is both added to and subtracted from the carrier. Another way of saying it is that the carrier frequency has been caused to increase and decrease by adding and subtracting the equivalent energy of the modulating frequencies. The net result is that after being modulated the carrier wave contains the original carrier frequency plus and minus the modulating frequencies. For example, if a carrier wave of 600 kHz (typical in the broadcast radio band) is modulated by audio frequencies of up to 5 kHz (typical audio frequencies), the resultant modulated carrier wave includes the original 600 kHz, as well as 5 kHz on either side of the carrier, or 5 kHz above and 5 kHz below. A band of frequencies has been created; 595 kHz to 605 kHz, with the center frequency of 600 kHz representing the original carrier wave and the 5 kHz of intelligence represented in the upper and lower sidebands of 5 kHz each, which are mirror images of each other. A radio signal is therefore a carrier with its sidebands (of information) (see Fig. 1-21).

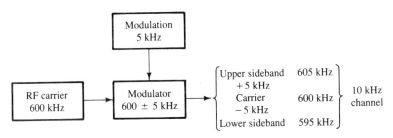

Figure 1-21   Sidebands.

Channels.   A radiated signal consisting of a carrier wave with its two sidebands are a group, or chunk, of frequencies. This fact requires that each transmitting station be allocated or assigned not merely one operating frequency, but a group of frequencies. Such an assignment is called a *channel*. It should be readily seen that the more intelligence (modulating frequencies) a carrier wave conveys, the wider the bandwidth that is generated, and the greater the channel space of the spectrum that it occupies. It is the FCC's job not only to assign which services are permitted to use carrier frequencies within a particular band, but also to designate the type of modulation permitted and the bandwidth (channel width) permitted or authorized any station within the service. Otherwise, adjacent stations could use differing kinds and amounts of modulation and could generate sidebands that would overlap another station's signal. Although the general public associates channels only with the television service, all stations in all services operate within channel assignments, which are very rigidly regulated.

Power.   After the modulated signal leaves the modulator, it (carrier with sidebands) goes through power amplifier stages where the signal in its entirety is made more powerful. The engineers determine how far they want the signal to travel (with the FCC's permission), calculate the propagation requirements, and design for the proper amount of power amplification. Generally speaking, the more stages of amplification that are added, the more powerful the signal that is delivered to the antenna for radiation. For very low power operations, such as a hand-held walkie-talkie, a small battery may suffice to provide the necessary amount of generating current. For a television broadcast station, the city power system feeds thousands of watts of electricity to huge oil-cooled transmitter stages to produce the necessary amount of signal power.

Transmission of the Signal

Overview.   The transmission process involves all aspects of the RF modulated signal propagation from the transmitting antenna to any or all receiving antennas. Transmission is controlled as much as possible to achieve the maximum radiated energy to arrive at the receiver(s) with a minimum of interference or distortion. The process is not entirely controllable, since radio waves are subject to natural phenomena and their own physical characteristics discussed previously. However, the process is optimized by using frequencies with desirable characteristics for the specific application, by designing proper transmitting and receiving antennas, by concentrating the radiated energy in limited directions when possible, by minimizing interference probabilities, and by manipulating any other controllable factors.

Transmitting Antennas.   Transmitting antennas, as discussed previously, must be designed according to the characteristics of the carrier frequency being radiated. Lower frequencies require tall metal towers of a full or fractional wavelength which radiate the signal. The middle frequencies generally employ metallic masts of the proper wavelength (which is much shorter) or fraction thereof, and are almost always mounted on top of tall towers as a better vantage point for their line-of-sight propagation. The higher frequencies are normally employed for point-to-point communications and employ parabolic dish antennas to concentrate the energy into focused beams aimed at the intended receiving antenna.

Propagation.   Reviewing propagation characteristics briefly, we recall that the different frequencies behave differently. The lower frequencies travel in ground waves, penetrating almost all obstacles, follow the curvature of the earth, and are used for reliable long-range service. Medium frequencies provide both a less pronounced ground wave, used for reliable medium range service, and sky waves that reflect off the ionosphere, providing skip waves for extremely long distance service. The highest frequencies travel in direct line-of-sight waves, tending to be absorbed or deflected by obstacles, ignoring the curvature of the earth and shooting off the horizon through the ionosphere into space. These frequencies are employed for short-range terrestrial services and for space communications.

Directional Antennas.   It has already been discussed how the extremely high frequencies, in addition to being radiated in all directions by a mast or tower antenna, can be focused into a concentrated beam and aimed. All radio signals, regardless of their frequencies, can be aimed to some degree or other. Antennas are made directional through reflecting techniques for the frequencies at the higher end of the spectrum, accomplished by variations of parabolic reflectors. However, parabolic dishes larger than football fields would be impractical for the lower frequencies, even if those long wavelengths would reflect. A more practical means of directional antennas for the lower frequencies is through phasing of the electromagnetic signals. Recall that magnets lying side by side with the same polar orientation push each other away, while those oriented with opposite polar orientations pull each other toward themselves; radio waves have similar characteristics. This same action applies when a second antenna of the same length as the main antenna is located an appropriate fraction of a wavelength distance away from the main antenna. When the signal from the transmitter is divided and sent to both antennas, but delayed slightly to the second antenna, the signal each radiates is slightly out of phase with each other. The antennas do not radiate their signals in synchronized polarity, but somewhat out of polarity. This polarity difference acts as two magnets lying side by side, but neither oriented exactly with the same or the opposite polarity of the other; they would tend neither to push or pull each other linearly as before. They would act as two magnets lying canted to each other, and their forces would push or pull each other in a canted direction. The net effect of the combined radiation pattern of the two antennas is to make a lopsided radiation pattern proportional to the phase difference between the signals in the two antennas. An antenna array of two or more phased antennas can be designed to produce rather sharply directional radiation patterns. This is a common practice in the AM radio service, where several towers will be employed as a single antenna array to achieve delivering the maximum amount of signal over the most populated areas (see Fig. 1-22).

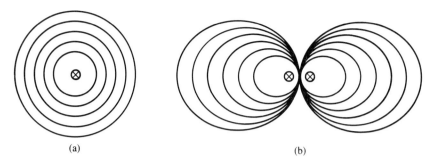

(a)   (b)

Figure 1-22 Directional antennas. (a) Omnidirectional (nondirectional) antenna pattern (top view); (b) directional (bidirectional) antenna pattern (top view).

Polarization.   Antennas can be placed on either vertical or horizontal planes and radiate equally as well. Visualize for a moment a small hand walkie-talkie with its mast antenna protruding from the top. The unit will radiate equally as well when held in a position on its side (with its antenna in a horizontal plane) as it will held upright (with its antenna in a vertical plane). Now, however, visualize the radio wave propagating from the antenna in each position. When in a horizontal plane (on its side), the propagated wave's polarity is oriented in a horizontal plane. A receiver some distance away will receive more energy of that wave if its receiving antenna also is oriented to the horizontal plane. More of the surface of the receiving antenna will absorb more of the wave's energy if it is oriented to the same plane than if it is perpendicular to it. Vertical receiving antennas will absorb more energy of a vertically oriented (polarized) wave than from a perpendicular wave. The generalization can be made that transmission efficiency is maximized when both transmitting and receiving antennas are oriented to the same plane, or have the same polarization (see Fig. 1-23).

Circular Polarization.   To eliminate the problem of many receivers having their antennas oriented in different planes, the antenna designers have produced transmitting antennas to radiate the signal in both planes simul-taneously. These are called *circular polarized antennas*, and receiving antennas will receive about the same amount of energy (signal) regardless of their orientation to the transmitting antenna. This certainly improves the performance of communication between a car radio with a vertical whip antenna and an FM radio station transmitting a horizontally polarized signal (see Fig. 1-23).

Interference.   As the radio wave is traveling from the transmitting antenna to the receiving antenna, it may be subjected to interference of different kinds. Natural interference and certain types of man-made interference have been discussed previously as threats to the radio wave. There are two other forms of man-made interference appropriate to be mentioned at this point. When the

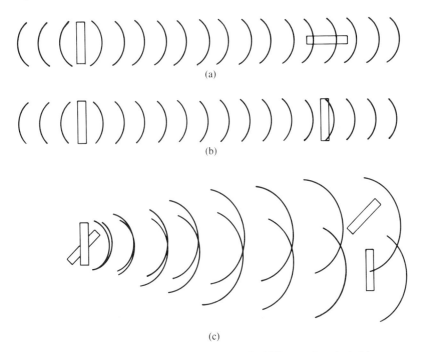

Figure 1-23 Polarization. (a) Minimum transfer (different orientation); (b) maximum transfer (same orientation); (c) circular transfer (either orientation).

signals from two different stations operating on the same carrier frequency collide, they can intermodulate and distort each other's waves, rendering the intelligence conveyed therein unintelligible. This is called *co-channel inter-ference* (two stations operating on the same channel whose signals interfere with each other). When the signals of two stations operating on adjacent (neighboring) channels are close and powerful enough, or when the permitted bandwidth has been exceeded, their frequencies will often overlap, distorting the signal of one or both. This also occurs when one station exceeds its assigned channel width, and its signal's sidebands spill over onto an adjacent channel signal. This is called *adjacent channel interference*. It is the FCC's responsibility in its regulatory scheme of authorizations and assignments to prevent this type of interference, but nobody is perfect.

Reception of the Signal

Overview.   For the purposes of the readers of this book, it is anticipated that the generation and transmission process of radio signals is of primary importance. These functions are the essence of the public interest in electronic communications as far as the regulators, lawyers, administrators, communicators, and managers are concerned. To understand those functions is to possess the foundation upon which to pursue a professional interest in the individual media technologies. The reception function is essentially the reverse of the previously discussed generation process, covering much of the same ground in reverse. Additionally, the internal workings of the receiving function are generally of interest only to the individual users of those receivers who expect them to work well, and to the design engineers and technicians who are expected to provide and maintain satisfactory operation. However, in the interests of completing a comprehensive discussion of the total communication model, and to tie up any loose ends, the discussion of reception will proceed lightly without belaboring the process.

The Receiver.   The function of the radio receiver is to sense the presence of radio waves on its antenna, to be able to distinguish or select a desired signal for processing, to amplify that signal to a usable strength, to detect and separate the intelligence from the carrier, and to display that intelligence appropriately. Part of the energy from the passing radio wave is absorbed by the receiving antenna and passed on to the tuner stage (RF selector), which can tune in and pass on a desired signal. The signal is then processed through amplifier stages to build up its strength to usable levels. It is then demodulated, stripped of its now useless carrier frequency, and the remaining intelligence sidebands are reconverted and displayed in their original forms: audio frequencies converted by a speaker into sound, video signals converted by picture tube into pictures, and data signals converted by various devices into appropriate data forms (for computer, teletype, etc.). The cycle is then complete (see Fig. 1-24).

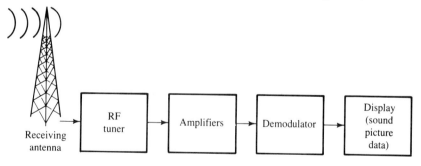

Figure 1-24   Basic receiver diagram.

Antenna Reception.   What has previously been said about the transmitting antenna is generally true of the receiving antenna, but is not as critical. The antenna will absorb the maximum of the desired radio wave energy if it is highly conductive (metallic), the same physical length as the exact wavelength of the carrier wave desired to be received, and is polarized (oriented) on the same plane as the transmitting antenna. The more that these requirements are compromised, the less efficient is the antenna. Also, the higher the frequencies involved, the more critical these factors become. Lower frequencies are more stable, predictable, and readily absorbed. Thus, the AM radio antenna on your car works adequately well in spite of the fact that it is not nearly as tall as the transmitting tower is. Yet, if you have a CB (citizens band) or FM radio in your car, which operate at much higher frequencies, the antenna length is much more critical.

Frequency Selection.   The variable (or fixed) radio frequency (RF) tuner of the receiver tunes its circuits to select one of the innumerable radio waves present in the antenna and passes it, with its sidebands, on to the amplifiers. The tuner might be viewed as an electronic gate: It opens just wide enough to pass the desired signal, and keeps all others out. Some receivers are designed with a fixed tuner that will receive only one predetermined channel. Others are variable over a range of spectrum and can be variably tuned to select any channel within that range.

Amplification.   The signal received by the antenna is very weak, an almost infinitesimal amount of energy (thousandths or millionths of a watt). The receiver has a system of amplification to build the signal back up to a strength adequate for processing to operate a display unit. As the signal passes through this amplification process, its strength is built up without distorting either the carrier or the sidebands of the signal.

Demodulation.   The signal is processed through the demodulator, which detects the intelligible variations within the sidebands by filtering out and discarding the now useless carrier frequency. The variations, which are the original electronic forms of audio, video, or data intelligence, are extracted, processed, and further amplified for reconversion to their original forms of energy.

Display.   The reconversation of these electronic versions of information into their original energy forms is the reverse of the conversion at the transmitter. Audio frequencies are fed to an audio speaker (which is a reverse microphone) for conversion back into the same originating sounds. Video signals are fed to a television picture tube for conversion back into the original visible pictures. Data signals are fed to a device similar to the one that generated them (computer terminal, teletypewriter, etc.) for conversion to the appropriate original display form. The intelligence has been faithfully conveyed from transmitter to receiver. The process is completed.

Summary.   All systems of radio communications are based upon a basic configuration of functions that is common to all. Whether the system is for radio or television broadcasting, microwave relays, or satellite communications, it must contain common functions interconnected in similar sequence. The overall purpose of the communications systems is to generate electromagnetic energy, to inject this energy with some form of intelligence, and to transmit this carrier wave with its sidebands to a distant location where the intelligence will be withdrawn from the carrier and utilized. The major components of the system are a radio transmitter with transmitting antenna and a radio receiver with receiving antenna. Within the transmitter, an RF carrier wave is generated and modulated with an electronic form of intelligence. This intelligence is representative of sound, pictures, or data which has been converted from its original energy form into electronic signals. These electronic signals modulate or mix with the RF carrier wave, and the composite wave (carrier and modulation sidebands) is amplified to sufficient power to radiate from the antenna for the distance desired. The receiving antenna absorbs a portion of the many radiated signals. Its RF tuner selects the desired carrier frequency channel and passes only that carrier (with its sidebands) for processing and amplification. The receiver's demodulator extracts the sideband intelligence from the now worthless carrier, and this electronic intelligence is reconverted back into its original energy form: sound, pictures, or data. This model is the basic structure of all radio communications systems.

the radio broadcast media

2

AM (STANDARD BROADCAST) RADIO

The Beginnings.   In the very early 1900s, radio telephony (voice radio as opposed to radiotelegraphy) was being experimented with by many engineers in many places. At the time, radio technology consisted of radio telegraphy used for point-to-point communications, and was in use mostly for maritime purposes and for military purposes during World War I. Between 1910 and 1920, technological developments occurred that permitted the marriage of telephone and radio technology. A radiotelegraph transmitter could be modified and connected with telephone technology to transmit the human voice. Thus was born the term *radiotelephony*. In 1920, an engineer experimenting with radiotelephony found it inconvenient to talk continuously on the air during experiments while transmitting to his assistant several miles away. He solved the problem by playing his phonograph over the transmitter while tinkering on the equipment. He soon became deluged with calls and requests to play favorite songs from listeners on their radios. The result was the establishment and operation that year of the nation's first radio broadcast station (and the first disc jockey).

Early Development.   In 1921, there were two stations on the air broadcasting to about 400,000 receivers. Within a year there were over 300 stations and more than two million receivers. Many of these "home garage" operations were operating with, and freely changing, sporadic power and frequency. To prevent chaos on the airwaves, the government (Secretary of Commerce) began regulating this broadcasting through a series of Radio Acts.

By 1925, the government had established that broadcast operations would be contained within the frequency spectrum range 550 to 1350 kHz of the MF band. This band was popular with the experimenters, and higher bands had not yet been conquered for practical use. Amplitude modulation (AM) was the designated type of modulation for the service, because no other form of modulation had yet been developed that could be used. It was also about this time that, as a result of several successful "commercial" operations, advertising was popularly accepted as the best way to finance broadcast operations. Shortly thereafter, stations began to interconnect their programming sources through telephone lines, and the radio networks were born. Due to these rapid and sophisticated developments, and to protect the public interest in all this activity, new regulatory controls were essential. To cope with these, and future developments, Congress enacted the Communications Act of 1934 and established the Federal Communications Commission (FCC). The rest, as they say, is history.

Technological Developments.   Early radio stations quickly developed from the garage-type facilities to large, formal operations with live programming (orchestras, actors, etc.), large studios seating live audiences, operated by large staffs. Plant equipment did not change so much in kind as it did in performance and power. The most visible technical progress was in increasing transmitter power. Prior to 1922, most transmitters operated at about 100 watts of power or less, but within three years the larger stations were operating between 1000 and 5000 watts. In 1927, the first station to attain a power of 50,000 watts went on the air, shortly followed by several others. Thereafter, the government put a ceiling on the maximum permissible broadcasting power at that level— 50,000 watts. At that time, however, the smallest stations were still operating at about 10 to 100 watts. Today, the maximum power limit for standard AM broadcasting has been retained at 50,000 watts, but the minimum has been increased to 250 watts to provide minimally adequate service to a significant population.

Receiver Development.   A significant impact on the development of broadcasting in the 1920s was the improvement of the radio receivers. Prior to 1925, receivers in the home were quite primitive and not designed for family listening. The listener had to wear a pair of earphones and painstakingly tune from station to station by manipulating and balancing the adjustment of three tuning dials. The receiver operated on batteries, and the circuitry provided listening quality that left much to be desired. Between 1925 and 1930, the headsets were replaced by loudspeakers, and triple-dial tuning gave way to single-dial tuning. The newly designed receivers had improved circuitry, providing increased performance, and the batteries were eliminated in favor of plugging the set into standard household electricity. When stations increased their power to cover wide ranges of population, and receivers became family-oriented, radio broadcasting was rapidly to become a predominant influence in American life.

Regulatory Perspective.   Present-day broadcasting is regulated under the Communications Act of 1934, as amended, by the Federal Communications Commission (FCC). Technologically speaking, the FCC mandate is to regulate broadcasting stations to minimize interference (co-channel and adjacent channel interference) between stations, and to provide standardized service (signals) to the public. Since this must be done on a national basis, and factors such as nighttime propagation changes (remember the ionosphere!) must be considered, technical regulation is highly complicated, minutely specific, and stringently enforced. Each station must be regulated as to which carrier frequency it can operate on, how wide its channel (sidebands or bandwidth) can be, and the amount of power it can produce. Stations are categorized for priority (predominance) of operation, are assigned hours of operation, are required to employ directional antennas where needed, and are assigned station identification (call) signs. When an applicant submits an application to build, license, and operate a radio station, he or she must submit engineering proof that it will not interfere with any other existing station in the country, and the FCC must verify this. And all of this in the days before computers!

The Present.   The basic technology of AM radio broadcasting is essentially not much different from the technology of the 1930s. True, many refinements and developments in techniques have occurred, but the original essentials are still the basis of broadcasting. Transmitters are more efficient, streamlined, stable, easier to operate, and smaller. Antenna design has evolved from the old self-supporting, free-standing tower to the modern slimline type supported by guy-cables. Directional antenna arrays have become very sophisticated and effective.

The most significant technological changes in AM broadcast stations are in their operational facilities and techniques. It is now common for studios and operations centers to be located in metropolitan business districts several miles away from the transmitter-antenna site located outside of the city or town. Transmitter and antenna control and monitoring are generally accomplished by sophisticated remote control systems. Programming often originates from these downtown studios and is sent to the distant transmitter by studio-to-transmitter (STL) links. Remote control and program distribution can be done individually or combined over telephone lines; however, it is increasingly common that these functions arc combined in a privately owned microwave STL system between transmitter and studio. Automation is used by many stations in varying degrees, from minimal to total; in business, programming, and transmitter operations. The most recent innovation to be approved and implemented is AM stereo. Because equipment has become relatively simple to operate, stable, and reliable, the FCC has been deregulating some of the operational aspects but not the technical standards of broadcasting.

The Name.   Often confusing, the term *standard broadcast service* is the official name of the AM radio broadcasting activities; the frequency band within which it operates is the *standard broadcast band*. This implies a false connotation that the FM radio and the television services are other than standard or broadcast. The name was assigned at the time when AM radio was the only broadcast service and was standardized therefore. Subsequently, FM radio and television were inaugurated as standardized broadcast services, but for some obscure reason the FCC never changed the official name of AM radio. Thus, "standard broadcast" and AM radio broadcasting are synonymous.

Overview of the Technology.   The standard broadcast (AM radio) service was established to provide a means of communicating information and entertainment to the general public. There are presently more than 4700 AM radio stations operating in the United States, and more than 170 more are presently being built. The government codified the state of the art as it existed in the 1920s, which resulted in the present-day parameters of technical requirements. The typical AM station operates on essentially the principles of the model communication system described in an earlier section. It is the FCC technical requirements that give the AM service a distinctive technical character from some of the other services. Since the FCC made AM what it is today, an understanding of it requires at this point more emphasis on the technical requirements than on a review of the model technology.

Frequency Allocation.   The frequency band allocated to the standard broadcast service is 535–1605 kHz. Since these frequencies are in the MF band, the service relies primarily on ground waves for communication. Recall that ground waves travel through the surface of the earth, following the curvature of the earth, and penetrate obstacles such as mountains, buildings, and the like. Ground wave communications are stable and reliable for medium-range communications. MF frequencies have a tendency, however, to produce a skip sky wave at night that can cause co-channel interference with distant stations operating on the same frequency. The ground wave of a typical station that travels 25–50 miles for its service area might produce a simultaneous night sky wave that travels 1000 miles to interfere with one or more stations in other parts of the country. This is a serious consideration in determining power and hours of operation assignments to individual stations.

Broadcast Band Allocation. The FCC determined that it would have to establish some kind of system to make station assignments so that they would not interfere with each other. Historically, the first stations were already operating within the MF band. The FCC therefore assigned the broadcast service to that band. To accommodate an adequate number of stations to provide service nationwide, the FCC allocated the frequencies of 535–1605 kHz to broadcasting.

Modulation Limits. Every carrier wave must be modulated with telephonic intelligence (sound, or audio frequencies). Sound, when converted by microphone or other transducer into electrical energy, has a frequency range of about 20 to 20,000 Hz (the audio frequency range). This constitutes the very lowest and the very highest tones that the human ear might hear in acoustical form. Since high fidelity sound recording or reproducing was unknown at the time, it was felt that normal voice audio frequencies would be adequate for broadcasting purposes. The FCC therefore arbitrarily (influenced by the limitations of the microphones of the day) assigned a limit of 5000 Hz (5 kHz) for modulation purposes. This was adequate to convey the recorded voice and music at the time.

Channel Width. Modulating an RF carrier with 5 kHz of audio frequencies will, as discussed earlier, produce a band of frequencies consisting of the RF carrier wave plus an upper and lower sideband of 5 kHz each, or a total signal width (carrier plus both sidebands) of 10 kHz. In other words, in order to carry 5 kHz of audio intelligence, the carrier wave would require a channel of frequency spectrum 10 kHz wide. Thus, the FCC must divide the assigned AM broadcast band into channels of 10 kHz each.

Channel Assignments. Since the broadcast band extended from 535–1605 kHz, it consisted of a total of 1070 kHz (1605 minus 535). Dividing that band into channels of 10 kHz (1070 kHz divided by 10 kHz) produced a total of 107 broadcast channels. Since each carrier has a 5 kHz sideband on either side of it, the carriers must be spaced 10 kHz apart to prevent the lower and upper sidebands of adjacent channels from interfering with each other. Thus, the lowest carrier frequency, in order to keep its lower sideband within the assigned broadcast band, must be assigned 5 kHz above the lowest frequency limit of the band—placing that carrier at 540 kHz. If the lowest carrier is assigned the frequency of 540 kHz and its upper sideband occupies 5 kHz above it, the next carrier frequency above can be assigned no closer than 550 kHz, making room for its lower sideband. Every carrier frequency must therefore be spaced 10 kHz apart. Thus, the FCC assigned 107 channels, 10 kHz wide, with their carrier (center frequencies) designated at 540 kHz, 550 kHz, 560 kHz, and every 10 kHz thereafter to the highest of 1600 kHz (which leaves room for the upper sideband of the 1600 kHz carrier). See Fig. 2-1.

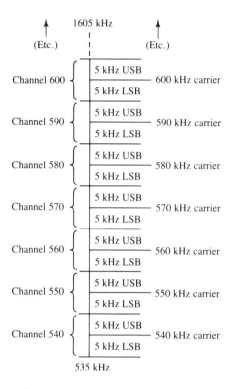

Figure 2-1 AM channel spacing.

Receiver Dials.   The dials on AM radio receivers are calibrated according to the channel numbers assigned, which reflect the carrier frequency. However, the dials of radios are too small to contain each entire frequency number (e.g., 1600 kHz), or even abbreviated numbers of all 107 channels. Therefore, the receiver manufacturers print only a sufficient number of channel numbers spaced across the dial to provide approximate channel tuning. Additionally, for space purposes, these channel numbers are often abbreviated to the smallest, still recognizable, number for identification. Channel 540 kHz (or 540) is printed on the dial as 54, channel 1000 kHz as 100, 1640 kHz as 164, and so on. The receiver must be tuned to the exact spot on the dial which represents the carrier frequency (the exact center of the channel), or distortion will result from a sideband of audio being partially excluded, and part of an adjacent channel's sideband creeping through (see Fig. 2-2).

Power.   At the time the government established comprehensive technical regulations for broadcasting, the strongest stations were operating with 50,000 watts of power. Feeling that this was sufficient to provide adequate coverage for rural areas, the government imposed this as the maximum limit for broadcast stations. Although many stations at the time were operating with as little as 10 watts or less, it was considered that such low powers were insufficient to properly

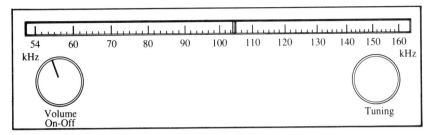

Figure 2-2 Typical AM radio receiver dial.

serve any significant geographic area. In the interests of standardizing a minimum service requirement for stations, 250 watts was established as the lowest authorized limit. This reasonably assured that even the smallest station would be able to provide service to at least an entire town. Thus, the limits of power that any individual station may be assigned are no less than 250 watts and no more than 50,000 watts.

Classes of Stations.   AM channels are assigned on the basis of coverage area and potential interference. Some channels are assigned to stations that are intended to provide wide areas of coverage, some regional areas, and some local areas. The FCC therefore established three classes of channels (and there are therefore three classes of stations). Certain channels designated as *clear channels* would accommodate powerful stations that would serve wide areas of cities, towns, and rural composition. These stations would have dominant status on the channel assigned, being permitted to operate up to a maximum of 50,000 watts. Other low-power stations would be permitted to share the channel, but would be geographically located and/or employ any necessary directional antennas required so as not to interfere with the clear channel (dominant) stations. Some channels are designated as *regional channels*. Stations assigned to any of these channels must provide service to a principal population center with its contiguous rural areas. Stations sharing these channels may be coequal, but must be geographically located so as not to interfere with each other. These stations are limited to 5000 watts of power. *Local channels* are designated to serve a city or town and its contiguous suburban/rural areas. Many low-power stations will share channels, but will be located so as not to interfere with each other. These local stations are limited to a maximum power of 1000 watts. (There are a very few special institutional-type stations still permitted to operate at 100 watts.) See Fig. 2-3.

Operational Hours.   Many stations share the same frequencies. Although they are geographically separated by adequate distances so that their ground waves do not interfere with each other, their nighttime sky waves often interfere with some of these other stations. Since this is essentially a nighttime

CLASS	POWER
Clear channel	10,000–50,000 watts
Regional	500–5,000 watts
Local	250–1,000 watts

Figure 2-3   Classes of AM stations.

problem only, a nighttime remedy must exist. To prevent this problem, the FCC determines which stations might generate nighttime sky wave interference to stations with a higher priority on the channel. These potentially offending stations are then licensed to operate only during daylight hours (local sunrise to local sunset), and must cease operation at night. Others are permitted to continue to operate at night, but with greatly reduced power. Those operating at night might also be required to employ directional antennas at night, or to use different directional patterns at night from their day patterns. This system of priority and protection maintains a reasonably (but not perfect) orderly AM radio service nationally, where otherwise chaos would reign supreme.

Antennas.   Antenna length is dependent upon the wavelength of the radiated signal. The AM broadcast band extends from 535–1605 kHz. At 535 kHz, the wavelength is about 1800 feet long. Even using a half-wave antenna of 900 feet, or a quarter-wave antenna of 450 feet is highly impractical. The only practical solution is to stand it upright (vertically), and to support itself it must become a steel tower (self-supporting or guy-wired). Even at the other end of the AM band, the wavelength of the 1600 carrier wave is about 600 feet, which requires a tower of 600, 300, or at least 150 feet. Towers this tall can prove to be a hazard to aircraft, so the FCC (and FAA) requires that the towers be painted orange and white and have lights for nighttime visibility. Directional antennas consist of several towers in an array, which can take up quite a bit of land acreage. Each tower in the array must be properly painted and lighted.

Polarization.   Since the physical dimension of the antenna must be vertical, the wave it radiates is vertically polarized. This is not critical, however, at MF frequencies because of the good absorption qualities of the MF energy. Therefore, the orientation of the receiving antennas is not critical. Receivers can as effectively use vertical antennas, horizontal antennas, or loop antennas (wire-wound antennas inside a receiver). This absorption quality of MF also makes the length of the receiving antenna not critical. Therefore, AM receivers can employ almost any kind of conductor as an antenna to receive local AM stations. For distant stations, however, vertical orientation and increased length of the antenna provide better reception of weak signals.

Summary.   The AM transmitter generates a carrier frequency, which is assigned in the MF band by the FCC, between 540 and 1605 kHz. This carrier is amplitude-modulated with an audio signal consisting of a range of audio frequencies up to 5 kHz. The modulation process generates sidebands of the carrier of 5 kHz above and below the carrier frequency. The upper side band (USB) and lower sideband (LSB) are mirror images of each other, and together constitute a bandwidth or channel of 10 kHz wide, with the carrier as the center frequency. This channel is amplified to a power authorized by the FCC (within a range of 250 to 5000 watts) and fed to a transmitting antenna. Antennas at these frequencies must be tall towers, several hundred feet tall. The ground wave of this signal follows the curvature of the earth and penetrates obstacles, providing reliable medium-range communications. To prevent the generated sky wave from interfering with other stations, many stations are permitted to operate only during the day, or with reduced power at night. Directional antenna arrays are also employed to prevent interference with other stations. Stations are categorized and assigned channels and power according to clear channel, regional, or local service functions.

AM STEREO*

Overview. Contrary to much popular belief, AM stereo is not a new concept—merely a new technology. The concept has been applied in various ways and times since the middle 1920s. The earliest efforts at AM stereo involved broadcasting an audio source over two separate AM transmitters operating on different frequencies. This necessitated that the audience listen on two AM receivers simultaneously, each tuned to a respective transmitter. Thirty years later, experiments with stereo involved AM/FM simulcasting. Typically, a radio station operating both a combined AM and FM station would broadcast the audio source over both stations simultaneously, the audience listening on separate AM and FM receivers simultaneously. The present technology permits the stereo signals to be conveyed by the same AM transmitter signal to a single AM stereo receiver. This signal is also compatible with existing receivers, which will receive it as a normal monophonic signal.

The Need. AM radio broadcasters have been understandably upset ever since FM radio began to overtake AM radio in the number of stations existing, listener ratings, and economic support from advertisers. As the first radio service, AM first looked upon FM stations as an adjunct service to their own, or an extension of their own. When FM stations went stereo and became a broadcast industry of their own, however, AM broadcasters became very unhappy over the siphoning-off of their audience and advertising. FM's high fidelity stereophonic music blossomed as the predominant attraction of listeners over AM's less than

---

*(For a detailed explanation of what stereophonic sound is and how it is achieved, see following section, "FM Stereo".

high fidelity monophonic music, news, and sports. AM broadcasters began to demand parity in technological capability.

The Reason.   The AM radio service was established at a time (the 1920s) when the leading edge of technology was involved with the medium frequencies (MF band) and had no reason to be concerned with high fidelity or stereophonic sound. After all, sound reproduction at the time was very primitive, relative to today's technology. As a consequence, for 60 years AM radio enjoyed the advantages of MF band propagation characteristics (ground wave), but also the limitations of modulation restrictions (narrow channels). When FM came along in the 1940s (having been invented in the mid-1930s), the only place available in the spectrum for this service was the VHF band, which has less desirable propagation characteristics (line of sight), but provided for the assignment of wider channels for modulation. Thus, although FM enjoyed the advantage of higher fidelity sound, AM enjoyed the advantage of stable longer-range propagation. Things changed in 1961 when the FCC authorized stereophonic broadcasting for FM, which was readily within the capability of the technology of that day, and the generous bandwidth of FM channels would readily accommodate it. Not so with AM, for which there was no technology available to squeeze a stereo subchannel into AM's very narrow channel widths.

AM Stereo Authorized.   Sound reproduction, both live and in the recording industry, was steadily and vastly improving in the 1950s, 1960s, and 1970s. FM music was sounding better and better. Stereo broadcasting gave it sparkle, depth, and presence. AM music sounded flat and dull in comparison. The radio audiences began leaving AM stations for FM stations. As this trend increased, and the technology became possible to shoehorn a stereo subchannel into an existing AM channel, the AM industry put the pressure on the FCC. In 1982 the Commission authorized stereophonic broadcasting for the AM service.

AM Stereo Limitation.   Although AM stereo will put AM stations in better competition with FM because of improved sound quality, it undoubtedly will never equal the quality of FM sound. Even if the stereo effect of AM equals that of FM, the fidelity (or full sound reproduction) of AM cannot match that of FM because of the channel width limitation. While the FM channel width can contain the entire audio spectrum ten times over, the AM channel width can contain only half the audio spectrum at best. Thus, although AM and FM can compete on a more favorable footing, FM will still have the edge on sound quality. Nevertheless, with AM's improved sound, its advantage in longer-range stability of the ground wave might tip the balance in its favor. This may be especially true with the automobile audience, for whom FM signals are often not of long enough range.

No Standard.   AM stereo has been slow to get started despite broad-casters' long and anxious efforts to get it authorized. There were, and tentatively continue to be, five different systems (different technologies) promoted by their respective manufacturers and supporters. Each system has its advantages and disadvantages, but they are not compatible with each other (although all are compatible with existing AM receivers). Anxiety and infighting rose to high levels as the industry awaited with bated breath the decision of the FCC as to which system would be designated as the authorized system, the standard. In May of 1982, the Commission decreed that it would sanction no specific system, but in the true spirit of deregulation would let the marketplace determine which system(s) would prevail. As a result, confusion and insecurity prevailed.

Slow Start.   Manufacturers began pushing their sales campaigns. Broadcasters, however, were reluctant to invest in any of these diverse systems. Each system works competitively well with the others; therefore, a system manufacturer's marketing strategy might determine which system would prevail. Each system required a different receiver; therefore, a receiver manufacturer's marketing strategy might prevail. The public would be confused as to which station operated with which system, and therefore would be reluctant to buy any specific receiver. If receiver manufacturers designed all-systems receivers, the cost might discourage the stereo audience. Or the confusion of another 5-position switch on the radios, and the resultant frustration over how to determine which position it needed to be in while listening to a particular station might discourage AM listeners. The risks were great, and therefore progress was slow in AM stereo's reaching the marketplace.

AM Stereo is Coming.   Nevertheless, stereo is coming to the mar-ketplace—slowly. Receiver manufacturers are building receiver multisystem sets for reasonable prices. The capability of automatic circuitry within the receiver to switch itself to the proper stereo system mode can eliminate the additional stereo switch and dispel listener confusion. It appears that, after a shaky and slow start, AM stereo will pick up momentum—in spite of the existence of the five different systems. The AM radio industry will (it is hoped) rise again!

Multiple Stereo Systems.   The FCC, in a display of questionable wisdom, decided that it would not determine a single standard for AM stereo technology. Instead, it would permit any manufacturer to design and market any system that could meet parameters of staying within the present assigned AM channel widths. Broadcast stations could buy stereo transmitting equipment from any of these manufacturers in order to broadcast stereo. While each of the systems is compatible with existing monophonic AM receivers (they will receive the stereo as a monophonic signal), they are imcompatible with each other. This means that persons with a standard monophonic receiver will receive the signals of all local AM stations as monophonic signals. Persons with a stereo receiver designed to receive only one stereo system signal will not receive the stereo of AM stations using the other systems. This confusion has caused much apprehension on the part of AM stations, and has been the reason for the very slow progress of AM stereo. (FM never suffered in this respect, since the FCC in those days very decisively established standards).

Receiver Capability.   Much of the confusion was caused by lack of knowledge of what receiver manufacturers would do. Some might design their receivers to receive only one system or another. Some might design a receiver to be switchable from one system to another (but how would the listener know which station was broadcasting which system signal?). Fortunately, the technology exists to design receivers that could sense from the received signal which system was employed by the station, and switch the receiver circuitry automatically to respond to that particular station's signal. That raises the question of cost of automatic multisystem receivers. The question remains as yet to be answered, but kits to enable existing receivers to receive the different stereo signals are becoming available for about $35.00 each installed.

Five Competing Systems

Although each of the five competing systems has distinctive features as well as advantages and disadvantages, it is not the purpose here to differentiate, compare, and evaluate them. It is merely the purpose here to establish that there is AM stereo technology and to briefly describe the general principles of the technologies involved, especially the similarities or principles they have in common. Since they all conform to the acceptable FCC parameters for AM broadcast channels, the technical distinctions, merits, and demerits will be left to the concerns of engineers.

The Systems in General.   The five systems are manufactured by Belar, Kahn, Harris, Motorola, and Magnavox. All of them are compatible with existing monophonic AM receivers. Each of them except the Belar system incorporates a stereo pilot tone accompanying stereo programming, which is intended to activate a stereo indicator light in the receiver, and can also be used to activate an automatic switching circuit. The pilot tone, a different tone for each system, can switch the receiver from mono to stereo function and also could cause the internal circuitry to switch to the proper stereo system reception (on receivers equipped with automatic multisystem switching). This pilot tone could also be used in the future to be modulated with digital codes to display the station's call sign or frequency on an alphanumeric display on the receiver.

The Kahn System.   The technologies employed by each system are not basically new technologies; they are generally standard techniques of various types of modulation in a new application. The Kahn system amplitude-modulates each of the carrier's two sidebands with a different audio channel. The transmitted signal consists of a standard AM channel but with independent sidebands, one carrying the left and the other carrying the right audio stereo channels. A standard monophonic receiver merely responds by demodulating both sidebands together, as usual, which results in their appearing simultaneously in the same speaker as monophonic sound. A receiver designed for the Kahn system will sense the pilot tone which will switch the receiver into the Kahn-stereo mode. The signal will then be processed through a detector which separates the sidebands, and each sideband is demodulated by a separate demodulator. The resulting separate audio signals are routed through separate audio amplifiers to separate speakers to produce the stereo effect.

The Belar System.   The Belar system employs a different type of modulation for each stereo audio channel. The following is a very general, oversimplified, and perhaps not specifically accurate description, but it provides the essential concept. The RF carrier frequency is amplitude-modulated with both audio channels, while the same carrier is frequency-modulated with just one of the audio channels. The resultant transmitted signal is a carrier frequency in the AM band, carrying both audio channels as amplitude modulation and also carrying one of the audio channels as frequency modulation. In an ordinary AM receiver, the AM audio signal is detected and demodulated, and appears in the speakers as monophonic sound—which it is. The FM audio channel is not processed at all, since the receiver has no FM circuits. In a receiver designed to also receive the Belar stereo signal, FM detection and processing circuits are built in. These detect and demodulate the FM audio channel. The AM and FM audio channels are fed into a matrix system in which that audio of the AM channel that is the same as the FM channel is cancelled out; thus, the outputs of the matrix are two separate audio signals representing the two distinct audio channels. Fed to separate speakers, they provide the stereo effect.

The Harris and Motorola Systems.   Both the Harris and Motorola systems are similar in that they use a phase differential of two identical RF carrier waves. Each uses a different amount of phase differential. (Perhaps a quick review of the section on directional antenna theory will help the reader to understand this phase differential.) Theoretically, an AM transmitter's RF carrier is amplitude-modulated with one channel of stereo audio. A second AM transmitter, operating on exactly the same carrier frequency, is amplitude-modulated with the other channel of stereo audio. The two modulated RF carriers are sent through a phasing device that combines them with their carriers shifted out of phase with each other (Motorola uses a 90-degree phase differential, while Harris uses a 30-degree differential). In actual practice, two separate transmitters are not necessary. A single carrier is split into two carriers, each modulated separately, and then recombined out of phase with each other.

This signal is received by standard AM receivers as a single signal, since the receiver has no phase-distinguishing circuitry. The two out-of-phase signals of the same carrier frequency are processed undistinguishable from each other, and all audio is in a mixed state at the output of the demodulator, providing monophonic sound. A receiver designed to receive the Harris or Motorola stereo signals, however, contains circuitry that detects phase differences. These circuits, detecting and separating the two out-of-phase carriers, cause the receiver to process each carrier through different AM demodulators, providing the distinguished stereo signals to separate speakers. The Harris and Motorola systems are not compatible with each other, because each uses a different phase differential.

The Magnavox System.   The Magnavox system is somewhat similar to the Belar system in that it uses two different types of modulation, one type for each audio channel. It is a bit similar to the Harris and Motorola systems in that one of those forms of modulation is phase modulation. The RF carrier is amplitude-modulated with both audio channels. The same RF carrier is then phase-modulated (which varies the phase of the carrier frequency at the audio rate) by a single channel of the stereo audio. When this composite signal is received by a standard AM receiver, the AM component containing both audio channels is processed and produces monophonic sound. The receiver contains no phase-modulation detection circuits and therefore the phase-modulated channel is not processed. In a receiver designed to receive Magnavox stereo, phase detection circuits demodulate the phased audio channel. The AM audio signal (containing both audio signals) and the phase-modulated audio signal (a single audio channel) are processed through a matrix circuit in which the phase-modulated signal cancels out its counterpart elements of the AM audio signal. The matrix outputs consist of the resultant two signals representing the original two audio channels to produce the stereo effect.

Synergistic Effects.   Recall that the AM channel bandwidth is 10 kHz wide, and that AM stations could modulate with only 5 kHz of audio because each sideband was a mirror image of the modulation audio. Therefore, 5 kHz of audio filled up the 10 kHz channel—unnecessarily. Since 5 kHz is only about one-fourth of the audio spectrum (which is 20 Hz–20 kHz), AM sound is flat compared to FM band audio (with the capability for full audio reproduction). Observe, however, that with the present technology for suppressing one sideband and separately modulating the other, and with modulating the same carrier with two distinct types of modulation, the AM channel can now be modulated with a full 10 kHz of audio. This doubling of its capability for fidelity, coupled with the added depth and presence of stereo, should provide AM broadcasting with a synergism that will rejuvenate the industry.

Summary. The high fidelity and stereophonic aspects of FM broadcasting drew the audience away from AM until FM's popularity surpassed AM. The FCC, in response to AM broadcasters' pressure, authorized AM stereo broadcasting, but unfortunately did not establish a technical standard. Consequently, five viable systems are competing with each other for the marketplace. Although each system is compatible with existing AM monophonic receivers, they are not compatible with each other. This has resulted in great apprehension over what the AM receiver manufacturers would do. As a result of the confusion and insecurity of broadcasters, AM stereo has been very slow in reaching the audience. With the advent of multisystem receivers, however, stations are beginning to commit themselves. This commitment should accelerate in the near future, since marketplace forces are trending toward establishing the Motorola C-Quam system as the de facto standard; however, the Kahn system is persisting. Harris has apparently withdrawn its system to support the Motorola system, while the Belar and Magnavox systems seem to be losing out in the competition.

The technology of AM stereo not only brings stereo sound but also improved fidelity to its listening audiences. These tremendous improvements, coupled with AM's inherent propagation advantage over FM radio, could rejuvenate AM as a viable competitor with FM radio again.

FM RADIO

Development. FM radio technology was developed in the early 1930s. Although it provided advantages over AM broadcasting, it was viewed as a threat by the AM broadcasters and was overshadowed by the developing medium of television. It had to struggle long and hard for its place in the sun. Just before World War II. the FCC assigned thirteen channels of choice frequencies low in the VHF band (42–50 mHz), and about thirty stations went on the air. During the war, further development was frozen for the war effort. After the war, the FCC moved FM's previous frequency allocation because of negative sky wave effects. It gave FM an increased allocation higher up in the VHF band. This action destroyed FM's existence at the time, because all FM receivers were then obsolete—they could not receive the new frequencies.

FM existed minimally thereafter because of AM broadcasters who obtained FM licenses as insurance in case FM caught on. These broadcasters merely duplicated (simulcast) their AM programming over the FM station. Finally, several things happened about 1960 to propel FM into its own identity. The popularity of better sound quality, the decreasing availability of AM channels, and a deliberate policy of the FCC to encourage FM development by restricting AM/FM simulcasting all opened the door for FM in the 1960s. Today, FM is surpassing AM radio in popularity with the listener. There are over 4700 stations on the air, and over 590 more are being built.

Advantages Over AM.   FM radio has several advantages to the listener over AM. Its frequency modulation and the wide bandwidths assigned give FM the ability for reproducing high fidelity sound, enhancing both music and voice. Where AM radio was limited to 5000 Hz of audio frequencies (tones), FM is capable of 15,000 Hz. This constitutes nearly the entire audible range, or audio frequency spectrum. Frequency modulation also provides a greater dynamic range of audio frequencies. This means much better reproduction between the softest and the loudest sounds. These two advantages make listening much more authentic and pleasurable. Additionally, FM is nearly free from static (electrical interference) for two reasons. Operating in the VHF band, these frequencies are significantly less affected by atmospheric interference. Static also primarily affects the amplitude rather than the frequency of a signal; thus frequency modulation is much less susceptible than AM. Finally, the circuit design of an FM receiver provides what is known as "capture effect." This means that once the receiver is tuned to a particular signal, it tends to "lock on" to that signal, preventing drift or a weaker signal from creeping in and distorting the signal tuned in.

Additional Capabilities.   FM channels were assigned wider bandwidths than necessary to carry the full audio frequency range (about 20 times wider than AM channels). This extra frequency space within each channel provides ample space to carry additional intelligence through a technique called *multiplexing*. This is merely a means of combining an additional intelligence component (or more) with the primary intelligence, to be carried simultaneously by the carrier wave, and separated for individual use by the receiver. The most popular use for this capability has been to send a second sound component (audio channel—or, more technically accurate, subchannel) with the first to produce stereophonic sound. Another use for this capability has been to provide a separate service to subscribers, who need a special receiver to receive the sound audio subchannel. This has long been used by stations for a second source of revenue by delivering background music programming (Muzak, or "elevator music") to businesses, stores, etc. This separate service using the same carrier wave is authorized by the FCC as Subsidiary Communications Authorization (SCA), and has the capacity for providing many new services. (This is discussed in a later section).

Table of Assignments.   Unlike the AM broadcast service, which assigns frequencies to locales upon a showing of noninterference, the FCC established a table of assignments for the FM service. This plan was devised to insure that all communities all over the country would be able to enjoy FM service. To this end, the FCC established a list of communities throughout the country and assigned channels to these specific communities. Persons applying for FM licenses must apply for one of the channels assigned to the desired community. If no channels are assigned to the desired community, or all are occupied, the applicant can petition the FCC to reallocate a channel from one community to another, based upon a showing of need to the community and noninterference with stations assigned by the established table of assignments. The table of assignments is published in the FCC rules.

The Model.   The functional model of an FM broadcast station is essentially the same as that of the basic and AM models explained previously. It consists of the generation, modulation, and propagation of a proper FM radio signal. Of course, the FCC determines the parameters for what constitutes a proper FM signal. This process requires a radio transmitter, audio intelligence, and an antenna.

The FM Band.   During the time when FM radio was being developed, the VHF band was the most available band for new services. Television was also a new service, and overshadowed FM. In the process of assigning choice VHF channels to television, the FCC arbitrarily sandwiched allocations for the FM service in between television channels, between TV channels 6 and 7. This FM band allocation consists of those VHF frequencies between 88 and 108 mHz. (See Fig. 2-4).

Channel Width.   The capability of FM to provide high fidelity sound, and the lack of serious concern at the time for frequency scarcity, prompted the FCC to provide each FM channel to be wide enough to carry adequate intelligence in the form of audio frequencies. Channel width for FM signals was thus established at 200 kHz wide. Since the entire audio spectrum is less than 20 kHz wide, it appears that a single FM channel could contain ten full audio spectra, or contain one full audio spectrum with about 180 kHz of empty space left over. (If this seemingly wanton waste seems a puzzlement to you, it has been to this writer for thirty years.) See Fig. 2-5.

Carrier Frequency Assignments.   Since each channel is 200 kHz wide, and this channel width must provide for equal upper and lower sidebands, the carrier frequency must be assigned as the center frequency of the channel. This provides for a carrier frequency with upper and lower sidebands of 100 kHz each. Therefore, starting at the lowest frequency of the FM band allocation (88 mHz), the first carrier frequency assignment must be 100 kHz (0.1 mHz) above it, or at 88.1 mHz. The next carrier frequency assignment above that must provide space for the upper sideband of the 88.1 carrier and for its own lower sideband. Since each sideband is 100 kHz (0.1 mHz), the next carrier assignment

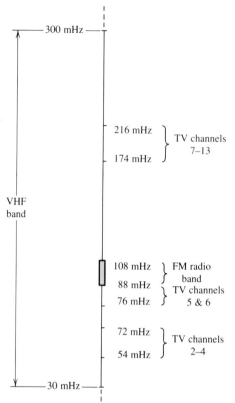

Figure 2-4 FM band allocations.

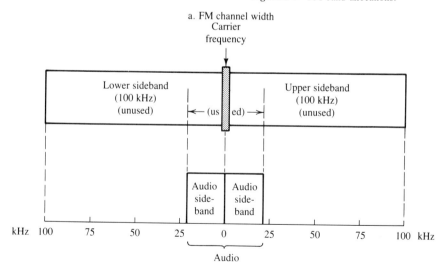

Figure 2-5 Used/unused portions: FM channel. (a) FM channel width; (b) audio spectrum.

is 88.3 mHz. Carrier frequencies therefore are assigned at every odd-tenth mHz, and spaced 200 kHz (0.2 mHz) apart throughout the 88–108 mHz FM band (see Fig. 2-6).

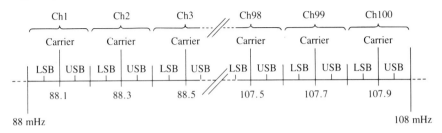

Figure 2-6 FM channel spacing.

Total Channels.   The entire FM band extends from 88–108 mHz. This is a frequency spread (or the band consists) of 20 mHz of frequency spectrum. Since each channel is 200 kHz (0.2 mHz) wide, the total number of FM channels is 100 (20 mHz divided by 0.2 mHz = 100 channels).

Educational Assignments.   At the time FM was developing, there was considerable thought among educators that radio held educational potential. There was concern, however, that the FM band, like the AM band before it, would be the exclusive domain of commercial broadcasting. To prevent this, and to provide for educational uses of radio, the FCC reserved (assigned) the lowest 20 channels of the FM band for noncommercial educational (or public) broadcasting. Stations operating on the FM band below the frequency of 92 mHz are operated by colleges, universities, public schools, and other nonprofit organizations (see Fig. 2-7).

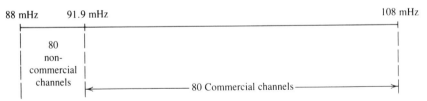

Figure 2-7 FM commercial/noncommercial channels.

Propagation.   FM is assigned to the VHF band, which has line-of-sight propagation characteristics. The stations' service area, therefore, is covered by direct wave. The FM service does not suffer from nighttime sky wave problems. Since the direct wave is line of sight, its maximum coverage area extends to the horizon. How far the horizon is away from the station depends upon the height of the antenna; the higher the antenna, the farther the horizon. At ground level the horizon is very roughly about 35 miles away, but a mountain-top antenna might triple that distance. Whether or not the signal can reach the horizon depends both upon the amount of power radiated and the surrounding environment (mountains, buildings, etc.). Thus, the stability and extent of the stations' service area is dependent upon antenna height, power, and topography.

Power and Antenna Height. FM stations are assigned to three different categories of power/antenna-height requirements. Class A stations are those intended to provide local service for populated areas. These stations are designed for a service radius of about 15 miles by limiting their power to between 100 and 3000 watts with a maximum antenna height of 300 feet above average terrain. Class B stations are those intended to provide service to a particular market area including a city and its surrounding suburbs and rural districts. To permit coverage of about 30 miles, the FCC limits the power of Class Bs to 5000 to 50,000 watts, and antenna height to 500 feet. Class C stations are regional stations serving large rural areas as well as their city of assignment. Their service range of about 60 miles radius is controlled by assigned power within a range of 25,000 to 100,000 watts, and a maximum antenna height of 2000 feet. No station in the FM service, therefore, is permitted a power greater than 100,000 watts or an antenna height greater than 2000 feet above average terrain (see Fig. 2-8).

Class	Service Area	Power Min. Max.	Antenna Height Above Average Terrain
Class A	15 mi.	100–3,000 watts	300 ft.
Class B	30 mi.	5,000–50,000 watts	500 ft.
Class C	60 mi.	25,000–100,000 watts	2000 ft.

Figure 2-8   Classes of FM stations.

FM Antennas.   The physical dimension of an antenna is dependent upon the wavelength of the carrier frequency transmitted. For the FM band of 88 to 108 mHz, the wavelength range is from about 11 feet (88 mHz) to about 9 feet (108 mHz). Therefore, the electrical length of any FM station antenna must be between 9 and 11 feet long. Antenna design technology produces some antennas that are rather strange in appearance in achieving efficiency and/or circular polarization. The FM antenna is almost always located on the highest terrain in the locale, and mounted atop a tall supporting tower. Very often the FM station leases space for its antenna on the tower of another AM or TV station. Generally speaking, all radio (which includes TV) towers are required to be lighted and painted with bands of orange and white for purposes of aircraft safety.

Polarization.   The typical FM antennas in the past were horizontally mounted and therefore were horizontally polarized, sending the carrier wave off oriented in a horizontal plane. This merely meant that the best reception by receivers was achieved with horizontal FM receiving antennas. These receiving antennas at the home often were incorporated into home TV antennas, or looked very similar, because FM and TV signals are both VHF and therefore the same approximate wavelength, and were horizontally polarized. In fact, since TV receiving antennas are designed to pick up all TV VHF signals, and since the FM signals fall within the TV band, television receiving antennas generally serve quite well for picking up FM signals.

All of the foregoing generally holds true today; however, there is an added dimension. Many automobiles and portable FM receivers cannot, for all practical purposes, employ horizontal antennas. The vertical (and usually telescoping) mast antenna is more practical. To provide a signal which can better be picked up on vertical antennas without sacrificing reception by the existing horizontal receiving antennas, FM stations use transmitting antennas designed to radiate the signal equally in both planes. These are called *circularly polarized* antennas, and work very well. Receivers tuning in a circularly polarized signal will receive it equally well with either a horizontal or vertical antenna (see Fig. 2-9).

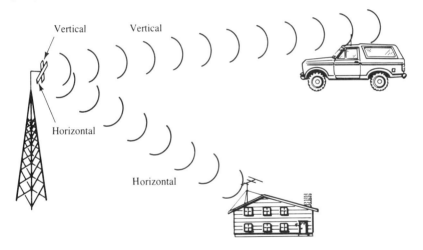

Figure 2-9 Circular polarization.

Summary.   The FM transmitter generates an RF carrier frequency. This carrier is then frequency-modulated (FM) with audio frequencies. Since the FCC has provided extremely wide channels for the FM service, the channel can accommodate modulation by the full audio frequency range with ample unused capacity to spare. This carrier with its modulated sidebands is amplified to the appropriate and authorized power and fed to the antenna. The FM antenna is mounted atop a tall supporting tower generally located on the highest elevation (hill or building) in the area. Propagation of this VHF wave is direct line of sight, limited to communications to the horizon.

The extent of its coverage area within this limitation depends upon the height of the antenna, the power of the signal, and the topography (terrain and obstacles) within the area. Circular polarization of the wave makes the orientation of the receiving antenna immaterial. Because of the nature of VHF waves, frequency modulation, wide channel assignments, and receiver circuitry, the FM service provides the listener with high fidelity reproduction virtually interference free.

FM TRANSLATOR

The Need.   The table of assignments established by the FCC is not a perfect device to insure FM service to all communities. Many communities ended up with no FM channel allocation in reliance upon neighboring community stations to serve them. Yet, in many cases, that neighboring service provides no local programming to serve the needs of the deprived community; or worse, the signal does not provide adequate coverage to include the deprived community. In other cases, although a community may have received an FM channel assignment, the community is too small to provide an economic base sufficient to sustain a radio station. Or a community may desire to receive a specialty (religious, foreign language, etc.) or educational station that operates in a neighboring community. For whatever reasons, there are often inequities or "holes" in the service provided by the table of assignments.

The Technology.   One device for correcting such deficiencies is the FCC's authorization for FM translators. There are presently nearly 790 FM translators in operation, with 450 more authorized for construction. An FM translator is merely a standard FM broadcast station that serves as a satellite (terrestrial, not spacial) or extension of another existing FM station. The translator is usually (but not always) owned and operated by the operator of the originating or parent station in another community. It merely rebroadcasts the programming of the originating station, but operates on an FM channel different from the parent station to prevent possible co-channel interference. The translator is a full-fledged FM broadcast station that must be in compliance with the FCC rules for all FM broadcast stations relative to signal standards. Since the translator usually provides service to a community smaller than that of the originating station, translators usually are assigned to operate at a low power.

Typical Scenario.   A typical scenario for an FM translator application might be as follows: The small town in a mountain valley enjoys the service of its local FM radio station. Just beyond the next mountain, a small mining community can receive virtually no FM radio signals because of the surrounding mountains. The community has no channel assignment to build its own station;

even if it did, no entrepreneur would risk the investment for such a small economic base. The owner of the neighboring town's FM station and the community petition the FCC for authorization and receive it. The manager of the neighboring station constructs a low-power FM translator (transmitter) near the deprived community at a vantage point where it can receive the weak signal from the station, demodulate the audio from its carrier, then use the audio to modulate the low-power translator's carrier frequency operating on another channel. (Another means would be to send the audio from the station's studio by telephone line to modulate the low-power transmitter, but this would not technically be a translator operation). The station manager then accepts advertising from merchants in the translator's community, and programs the station (and therefore the translator) with occasional news and information of interest to the translator's community. The translator has thus extended the range of the station, bringing FM service to the community as well as more revenue and prestige to the station. The station, the town, the community, and the FCC are all happy (see Figs. 2-10 and 2-11).

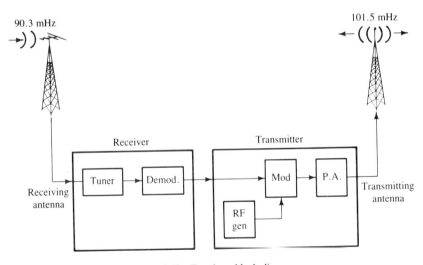

Figure 2-10   Translator block diagram.

Summary.   The FM translator is an unmanned, automatic, low-power, standard FM receiver/transmitter employed to extend the range or coverage of a parent or originating FM station. Located at a distant site to serve another community, the translator receives the weak signal of the originating station and rebroadcasts it locally on another standard FM channel. Translators employ the same technology and must adhere to the same technical regulations as standard FM broadcast stations; however, they do not originate programming. They operate merely as an extension service for the programming of another station.

Figure 2-11   Translator application.

FM MULTIPLEXED SERVICES

Overview.   The FM service provides channel widths that are not fully utilized by the normal transmission of sound (audio). The process of modulating the FM carrier wave with an audio signal of 15 mHz leaves a lot of empty capacity in the channel. This process of using the carrier to transmit a single form or channel of intelligence for a single purpose is called *simplexing*—the simple transmission of a single signal. Since technology first developed this simplexing process, it has further developed the means to send additional and separate intelligence (or signals) within the same FM channel. This requires the creation of a subcarrier within the channel and modulating it with a separate distinct intelligence signal. This is akin to two transmitters operating within the same channel but on slightly different carrier frequencies, and transmitting their composite signal together. Reception of this composite signal requires receivers designed to receive either one or the other carrier (carrier or subcarrier), or both simultaneously, depending upon the use of the signals conveyed. This form of creating a single complex channel to convey two or more separate and distinct message forms is called *multiplexing*.

Multiple Multiplexing.   The multiplexed process can create as many subcarriers (and therefore subchannels) within the assigned channel as there is frequency space to accommodate the intelligence modulated upon them (and which the FCC will permit). In the case of FM channels, if the carrier is modulated with 15 kHz of audio, this modulation occupies a 15 kHz upper sideband and a 15 kHz lower sideband, or 30 kHz of channel space. The channel is 200 kHz wide; therefore, there remains 170 kHz of unused channel space. If a second audio or other signal is desired to be carried separately, a frequency within the unused 170 kHz area can be amplified and modulated, creating a subchannel. Whatever frequency space is still unused, one of its frequencies can be amplified and modulated with a third intelligence signal, creating a third subchannel. Additional subchannels can be created for distinctly separate intelligible modulation until all the channel space for this single channel is filled up.

Uses. This multiplexing technique is especially practical in the FM band with its extremely wide channel assignments with unused capacity. It has been used by many stations for years to deliver Muzak music to subscribers with special receivers to receive only the subcarrier program, while broadcast listeners with normal sets hear a completely different program with commercials on the main channel (carrier). Stereophonic broadcasting is accomplished by this technique, sending two separate audio channels to the same receiver. When multiplexing is done to permit the FM broadcaster to offer a secondary service to nonbroadcast paying subscribers with special receivers, this operation is authorized and controlled under the FCC's Subsidiary Communications Authorization (SCA). These FM multiplexed services are discussed in the following sections.

FM STEREO

Definition. In 1961, the FCC authorized stereophonic broadcasting by the FM service. Stereophonic (stereo) sound gives a three-dimensional quality to recorded and reproduced sound, or a *live* sound. The primary effect of stereo may be illustrated by sitting in a room listening to recorded music with your eyes closed. If the reproduction is high-quality stereo, it will appear in your imagination that the orchestra is in front of you and seems so live that you can point to exactly where the different musicians are sitting. If you cannot, no matter how good the music sounds, it is either poor stereo or monophonic (mono) sound. Even if the music is emanating from multiple speakers located at various points in the room, if the realism is not present to enable the listener to "locate" (envision) each musician's position, it is merely diffused sound, not stereo.

Live Stereo. Stereo produces a live sound, meaning that when it is reproduced, it sounds as though you were listening to the actual source at the time of the recording, or are present at a live broadcast. When you are listening to actual live sounds, you have a sense of "presence" of that sound. Your ears give you the sense of depth and direction of sound, just as your eyes give you depth perception and direction of sight. When your ears each receive the same sound at exactly the same moment and exactly the same strength, you know that sound is directly in front of you. You also receive a certain sense of sound depth perception from this sensation. As you turn your head to either direction, or as the sound source moves to either direction, each ear receives the sound at a slightly different instant and strength. Your sense and experience provide a sensation of the changing direction and distance. Thus, with your eyes closed, you can determine the direction and approximate distance of the sound source. When two or more different sounds are listened to simultaneously, you sense where each is coming from. The two ears working in conjunction with each other provide a sense of direction and depth for sounds.

Recording Stereo.   For a listener of recorded or broadcast music, the ears must hear the same sounds in the same way as if he were present at the live source in order to sense the stereo effect. Therefore, since the sensation depends upon what each ear hears individually, there must be two separate channels of the reproduced sound, one representing each ear. To demonstrate, assume that a musical trio is being recorded live. Two microphones must be used, one representing each ear, and placed in front of the trio, separated by the equivalent distance of the head. The two microphones pick up the sounds (both direct and reflected sounds) from each musician in slightly different times and strengths, as would human ears. The resultant output from the right microphone is recorded separately (right channel) from the output of the left microphone (left channel). When the two separate recorded channels are played back (by record player, tape or broadcast), the two channels must be separately connected to individual speakers, located close together, the right channel speaker being to the right of the listener, and the left channel being to the left of the listener. As the recording (or broadcast) is played, the listener hears with his own ears the combined output of the two speakers reproducing exactly what each of his/her ears would have heard during the live recording (or broadcast). The exact same sounds produce the exact same sensations as if it were live, giving the listener the exact location and distance of the musicians during the original recording or broadcast (see Fig. 2-12).

Broadcasting Stereo.   To achieve stereo broadcasting, the broadcast signal must be able to carry two separate and distinct audio signals (or audio channels). [The terminology can get confusing at this point, because when we are talking about the audio signals we refer to them as *channels*. When we talk about them within or as part of the broadcast signal (as sidebands), we refer to them as *subchannels*. They are separate channels of sound, but subchannels of the broadcast channel (signal)]. Additionally, the radio receivers must be able to process two separate audio channels. The FM service provides channels wide enough to carry more than two audio channels. However, such a complex signal would seem not to be receivable by ordinary FM receivers. The FCC required that an FM stereo signal must be compatible with both existing monaural and stereo receivers.

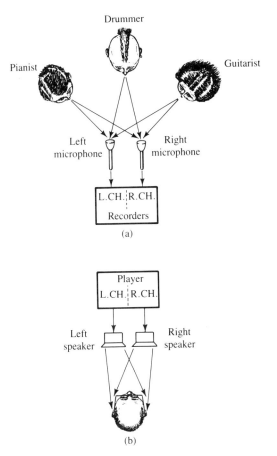

Figure 2-12   (a) Stereo recording; (b) stereo reproduction.

Multiplexing.   Stereo is achieved by the process of multiplexing. It would be easy enough to provide a stereo signal by modulating the carrier frequency with one audio channel, then selecting a second frequency, still within the FM channel width but a full audio spectrum away from the carrier, and modulating it (a subcarrier) with the second audio channel. This arrangement could be accomplished by building two transmitters in one, generating two carrier waves an audio spectrum apart, modulating each carrier with a separate audio channel, then sending both carriers simultaneously from the same antenna. This compound signal could be received by a standard FM receiver, which tunes broadly enough to receive the whole channel. Both audio subcarriers would be detected and demodulated, and the audio from both would be sent through the normal single audio amplifier and speaker, presenting the two mixed signals together as monaural sound. Special FM receivers could be designed to receive the entire channel, but then internally separate and channel the carrier and the subcarrier into separate processing demodulators, audio amplifiers, and speakers. This would produce the separate channels of sound required for the stereo effect. This system provides a stereo signal compatible with both stereo and monaural receivers. The preceding description is a gross oversimplification of the stereo multiplexing process, but, if understood, it should suffice for the purpose of most readers of this book (see Fig. 2-13).

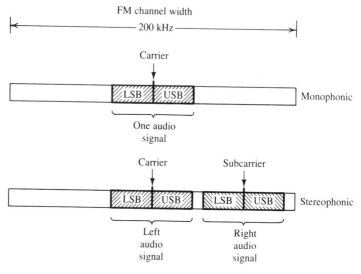

Figure 2-13   Basic stereo multiplexing.

Multiplexing Intricacies.   To satisfy my own conscience and to maintain integrity with technologists, I shall expound very briefly on the procedural intricacies of the electronic process. (The rest of you may skip this paragraph). In actual practice, the channel carrier wave is modulated with both left (L) and right (R) audio signals, each of which is out of phase with the other. The subcarrier is modulated with just one of the audio signals (such as the right—R). A pilot subcarrier (unmodulated) is placed between the carrier and the subcarrier frequencies as an electronic reference for receiver circuits. As this complex wave is received by the standard monophonic FM receiver, only the main carrier with both L and R audio signals is demodulated; both audio signals are sent through the common audio amplifier to the common speaker system, and are reproduced as normal monophonic sound. (It does not possess circuits that can detect the phasing differences between the carrier and subcarrier modulation.) In a stereophonic receiver, however, a special phase detector circuit admits the proper phased left channel signal from the main carrier while rejecting the improperly phased right channel. The right channel audio from the subcarrier is demodulated by another circuit. The separate left and right audio signals are then sent through separate audio amplifiers and speakers to produce the stereo effect. Incidentally, one of the functions of the pilot subcarrier is to turn on the little red "stereo" light on receivers so equipped to visibly signal that stereo is being received; the other is to activate the phasing circuits of the receiver to place it in stereo mode of operation (see Fig. 2-14).

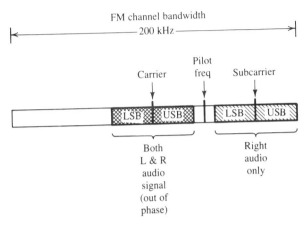

Figure 2-14   Actual stereo multiplexing.

Summary.   To transmit stereo sound, the FM transmitter must have dual functions to transmit two separate audio signals within its normal channel. Generally speaking, the transmitter generates two carrier frequencies within its channel—the main carrier and a subcarrier. Each of these is modulated separately by a different audio signal (a left and right audio channel). This composite waveform is transmitted to the receiver. Within the standard monophonic receiver, the circuits do not distinguish between the two carrier waves; they demodulate all audio (both audio signals) and send it through its single audio amplifier and speaker system. The result is monophonic sound. The stereo receiver, however, is designed so that its circuits operate as two separate receivers; each processes a carrier or subcarrier separately. Thus, the two audio signals are separately demodulated and sent to separate speakers. This faithful reproduction of separately recorded audio signals provides the listener with the sensation of live presence of the sound.

SCA (SUBSIDIARY COMMUNICATIONS AUTHORIZATION)

Overview.   Multiplexing of the FM channels has long been used for the broadcaster's own use in remote control and instrumentation of the broadcasting operation itself. It is only very recently, however, that the FCC, in its continuing quest for spectrum efficiency, authorized multiplexing to be used by the broadcasters for nonbroadcast services. Thus, the broadcaster can use his subchannels to serve the public at large, limited segments of the public with special interests, and individual firms, organizations, and persons. They can be used for providing such services as paging, inventory control and distribution, price and delivery, information, bus and truck dispatching, and police communications. This service is officially known as the Subsidiary Communications Authorization (SCA).

The Service.   In changing its rules to authorize nonbroadcast-related uses of FM subchannels, additional communication services are provided without the need for additional allocations of valuable spectrum. Subcarriers become available when FM stations utilize multiplex techniques to divide the usable channel spectrum into main channels and subchannels. Although the intelligence carried on a subchannel is not necessarily related to the main channel, the subchannel itself is part and parcel of the bandwidth each FM station is authorized to use. Thus, channels of communication are available and can be used only if the FM broadcaster chooses to do so. However, in the interests of spectrum efficiency, the FCC promotes the utilization of SCA services. Using spectrum that was originally allocated to the FM service, broadcasters may provide additional communication services without materially affecting the provision of their main channel programming.

The Technology.   The technology of SCA is identical to the multiplexing process described previously for stereophonic broadcasting. The FM transmitter generates its assigned carrier frequency, which it modulates for "main channel" monophonic broadcasting. If stereo broadcasting is incorporated, the transmitter modulates a second or subcarrier with a separate audio signal, creating a subchannel for the stereo signal. Whether or not stereo is being broadcast, the SCA service modulates a different or third subcarrier in the unused channel area with a completely different intelligible signal. SCA can use any form of modulation. This creates a separate subchannel intended to be received by persons with special SCA receivers for nonbroadcast services. Normal FM broadcast receivers cannot "hear" the SCA signal, and SCA receivers cannot hear the main channel or stereo programming. However, special receivers can be designed to selectively receive one, the other, or both broadcast and SCA programming.

FAX (FACSIMILE)

Overview.   Facsimile is another of the multiplexed services of FM broadcasting, rather than a new technology itself. This is a method of using an FM subcarrier to transmit visual still frames, or pictures. FAX can be used to convey copies of photographs, maps, documents, or any other still picture that does not contain highly intricate detail. It is included as a separate topic in this treatise (rather than included as an SCA service) because it has specific technical parameters assigned and has been considered a separate service, and because the possible future developments of this service may be significant as a distinct service.

The Process. FAX uses a subcarrier of an FM channel in precisely the same way that the stereo signal and the SCA signal are transmitted. A picture is scanned in fine horizontal lines by a photoelectric device. The device, as it scans, generates an electrical current according to the darkness of the picture. The darker areas of the picture generate correspondingly stronger current, while white generates almost no current. The scanned areas of the picture produce an electrical signal representative of all shades of black, gray, and white. This electrical signal modulates the FM subcarrier, along with a synchronizing signal that clocks the rate of speed of the scanning device. The modulated subcarrier is received by a special subcarrier receiver that is connected to a printing device that scans a page of special blank paper at the same rate of speed and same number of lines as the originating scanning device. As the signal is received, the synchronizing portion of the signal paces the printer to scan in synchronization with the transmitter scanner. While scanning, the printer responds to the demodulated picture intelligence. These FAX signals cause the printer, while scanning across the paper exactly as the transmitting scanner is doing, to electromechanically turn the paper dark, gray, and white in exact compliance with the picture signal. The result is an exact copy of the picture scanned at the transmitter, done electronically. A typical transmission requires about ten minutes to produce a picture of the quality of a single frame of a television picture, but on paper rather than the face of a TV picture tube.

The Potential. As indicated previously, the future of FAX may hold much greater use than present. It is not limited to the multiplexed technology of the FM broadcast service. It can be used as either a primary service or multiplexed service by private radio, common carrier radio, marine radio, and the like. It is presently being used, among other ways, by various countries to send updated weather charts or maps to ships at sea from shore-based radio stations, often relayed to ships by geostationary satellite. Refinements in the technique to produce higher-quality picture at faster rates, and developments in the delivery system via satellites make FAX an interesting technology worth watching.

the television
broadcast media

3

BROADCAST TELEVISION

Early Development.   Television, or "flying pictures," was envisioned by theorists in the 1800s. In fact, by 1923 there were patents for an all electronic, albeit crude, system. This system, however, was in competition with a mechanical system for converting pictures into electrical transmission. While the electronic system foundered in technical problems and patent lawsuits, the mechanical system progressed. By 1928, actual television transmissions were made by the mechanical system as transmitted in the LF band in the United States. By 1933, Germany was regularly broadcasting with this crude system. During the 1930s, however, technical developments were made in the United States by a team of industry engineers who produced a workable all-electronic system. This system was demonstrated (experimentally) at the New York World's Fair in 1939.

In 1941, the U.S. television industry agreed on technical standards for the system (a black and white system, since color was a long way off). The FCC authorized 13 channels in the VHF band for this service. (Channel 1 was later taken away from TV and given to another service.) Before any significant industry could develop, however, World War II interrupted further expansion and development. Six experimental stations remained on the air during the war, so activities did not die out completely. After the war, a state of confusion existed in the television industry for a while, which delayed expansion. During this period, nevertheless, two developments occurred to later spur progress: (1) There was significant improvement in the device to convert light to electricity for cameras. (2) AT&T began stringing intercity video coaxial cables necessary for network interconnection of television.

The Rules Developed.   Suddenly, the number of television stations increased from 17 to 48. The number of cities served increased from 8 to 23. In one year, the audience increased by about 4000 percent. It became apparent that 12 channels would not handle the demand for national television service. In 1948, the FCC imposed a five-year freeze on television development while it studied the problems and pondered solutions. In 1952, the FCC issued new rules for television which added 70 new UHF channels to the existing 12 VHF channels for a total of 82 television channels. (Years later, the FCC would take the highest 14 channels away from the TV service and allocate them to another service, leaving TV with 68 channels.) Additionally, the channels were assigned to communities to provide for national TV coverage according to a predetermined plan. Some of these assignments were reserved for educational, or noncommercial, use. This table of assignments has been, and continues to be, amended many times.

Immediately after the new rules were published in 1953, the number of TV stations tripled. This momentum was further accelerated when a compatible color standard was established by the industry the same year. However, because of the early high cost of color TV production and the high cost of color sets, color TV did not really become established until about 1972, when half the U.S. homes had color sets. Today, there are nearly 1200 TV stations operating in the United States, with about another 275 more authorized for construction.

UHF vs. VHF.   A word must be said here about the differences in the development between VHF and UHF stations. The 1952 allocation of channels to communities intermixed VHF and UHF channels in the same market area. This put UHF stations at a decided disadvantage. Because of the inherently shorter propagation characteristics of UHF waves, UHF transmitters are more expensive to install and operate. For over ten years, TV sets had no UHF tuners, and an external converter box had to be used for receiving UHF. It was not until 1964 that the government required manufacturers to incorporate UHF tuners within the sets. Even then, the manufacturers built the UHF tuners as continuous dial-type tuners, which were very difficult to tune exactly on a channel. This was not resolved until the late 1970s, when the FCC required "click-stop" tuners. Another problem was that the networks had already affiliated with stations on the original 12 VHF channels in most markets, and certainly had no incentive to affiliate with the disadvantaged UHFs instead. For these reasons, the number of UHF stations surged briefly until 1954, when they declined to approximately half their number by 1960. They started a slow growth in 1965, but continued as money-losers until about 1974, when many started to show a modest profit margin. Many inequities continue to exist today, but UHF is alive and well, although not nearly as well as VHF.

Table of Assignments.   The present-day allocation of channels to communities, or table of assignments, is based upon the overall plan of national coverage established during the freeze of 1948–1952. The FCC at that time laid out a master plan to provide that every community in the country would be served by at least one TV station. Thereafter, the plan called for additional assignments to communities to provide that more densely populated areas would be served by an appropriate, or proportionate, number of additional stations. In other words, the largest cities would be served by the most number of stations (six to ten), the smallest communities by at least one, and those communities in between by a proportionate number. According to this plan, it was necessary to establish a matrix of assignments dictated by adequate geographic separation of co-channel and adjacent channel stations to prevent interference. This had to be done for each of the (then) 82 channels; various permissible powers, antenna heights, and the like also had to be considered. This table of assignments (changed frequently) is published in chart form, showing each assignment by community and channel number(s), in the present FCC rules.

The TV Bands.   The FCC originally assigned the television service to the VHF band. To provide adequate frequency bandwidth for each channel to contain all of the necessary intelligence required for picture, synchronizing, and sound information, the Commission determined that each channel would be 6 mHz wide. It also initially decided that 12 channels would be sufficient for the service, later eliminating channel 1 due to interference problems. Since these 12 channels were each 6 mHz wide, there was no chunk of contiguous frequencies in the VHF band to accommodate the channels. Therefore, the channels had to be, in some cases, sandwiched in between frequencies being used by other services. Thus, channels 2, 3, and 4 were assigned to 54–72 mHz. Channels 5 and 6 found themselves at 76–88 mHz. Channels 7 through 13 were assigned the chunk of 174–216 mHz. Subsequently, when the FCC realized that the VHF channels would not be sufficient for the national coverage plan, it decided to add 70 more channels. Since each of these channels also required 6 mHz of band space, and since there was not sufficient VHF band for them, these channels were assigned to the UHF band. That band had sufficient contiguous unused frequencies for all 70 channels to be assigned contiguously. Since that time, the Commission has transferred the highest 14 of those channels to another service. The 56 UHF channels 14 through 69, therefore, occupy the frequencies of 470–806 mHz. The television service is assigned a total of 68 channels (see Fig. 3-1).

Transmission Overview.   The television transmission process employs two distinct transmission systems: a visual transmitter and an aural transmitter. The visual transmitter operates as an AM radio transmitter, but modulates the RF carrier with video signals from studio cameras and other video sources. The visual signal is then power-amplified and sent to an appropriate

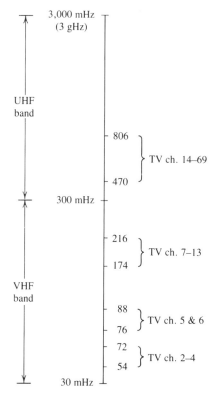

Figure 3-1 The TV bands.

antenna. The aural transmitter operates as a typical FM radio transmitter. It modulates an RF carrier with audio signals from microphones and other audio sources. The aural signal is then power-amplified and sent to the same antenna as the visual signal. The two RF carriers (visual and aural) are far enough apart in frequency so that their sidebands will not interfere with each other, yet close enough together so that the broadly tuned channel selectors of TV sets can receive both simultaneously as parts of one single channel, or signal. When the TV set tuner is turned to any "click-stop" channel setting, the tuner circuit is broadly designed to receive the desired visual carrier and its companion (associated) aural carrier. Receiving both simultaneously, the TV set takes for granted that it is receiving a single TV channel of picture and sound (see Fig. 3-2).

Reception Overview.   The television receiver is actually two receivers in one. It consists of an AM receiver for the visual signal and an FM receiver for the aural signal. The TV signal is generally picked up by a broadly designed antenna that responds to a wide range of frequencies or channels. The channel selector (tuner) of the receiver selects a desired channel setting which permits the

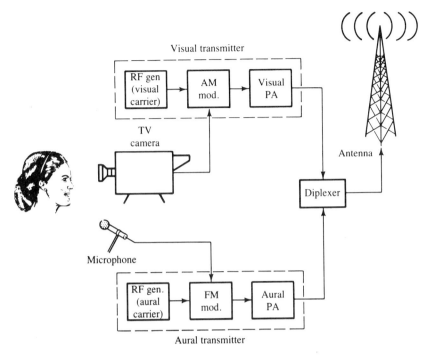

Figure 3-2 TV transmitter block diagram.

appropriate visual and aural signals to enter the receiver. They are separated and processed by the appropriate receiver section. The demodulated video information is applied to the TV picture tube, which reconstitutes the original picture. The demodulated audio information is applied to the TV set speaker for reproduction of the original sound. Since visual and aural signals were originated, transmitted, and received simultaneously, they accompany each other in exact synchronization (see Fig. 3-3).

Picture Conversion. The television camera is aimed at a pictorial scene. The light reflecting from that scene is focused by the camera lens onto the glass face of a photosensitive pickup tube in the camera. The inside of the face of the tube is coated with a light-sensitive material that responds electrically to light. Areas of the coating that strong light falls upon assume a strong electrical charge. Areas of weak light produce weak electrically charged areas. Areas of no light produce no charge. Thus, the electrical charge at any given infinitesimal spot on the coating at any moment is in direct proportion to the amount of light projected on that spot by the lens. An electrical image exists on the tube face.

Within the pickup tube, an electron gun scans the coated face of the tube. This scanning process is electronically controlled to scan across the face from left to right and top to bottom in very fine horizontal lines. The scanning process

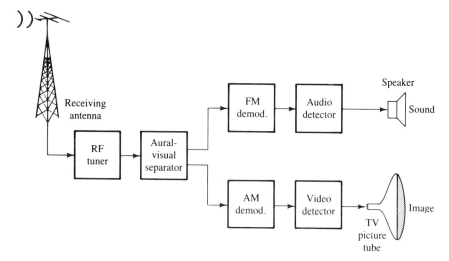

Figure 3-3 TV receiver block diagram.

is continuously repeated. While scanning, the electron gun senses the electrically charged areas of the face, producing an electrical current in direct proportion to the charged areas as it scans. Each time it completes a scanned picture, it starts over to scan a second picture. This scanning process produces a constantly flowing electrical signal, representing at any given moment the brightness of an element of the picture or image. Thus, the pictorial scene has been disassembled and converted into electrical signals which, if the process were exactly reversed, could reproduce the picture exactly, but in black and white only. Since the scanning process is continuously repeated many times per second, motion in the scene is reproduced by a series of extremely rapid successive images, as in the motion picture film process (see Fig. 3-4).

Color Mixing.   The electronic system has not been developed that can detect and reproduce all color directly. The best way that has been achieved is the ability to electronically break down pictorial scenes into three primary colors, transport these three colors in electronic form, and reconstitute the scene by mixing these primary colors in the original proportions to attain the original multiple colors. The basic technique of artists to be able to mix varying amounts of the primary colors of red, blue, and yellow to create any other color is well known. This technique is used in color television, with a slight difference. The primary colors of red, blue, and yellow work well in the subtractive process of pigmentation, but in the pure additive process of electromagnetic mixing (color is electromagnetic energy), the primary colors must be red, blue, and green. Therefore, in order to accomplish color separation and mixing in television, every pictorial scene must be broken down into its primary colors of red, blue,

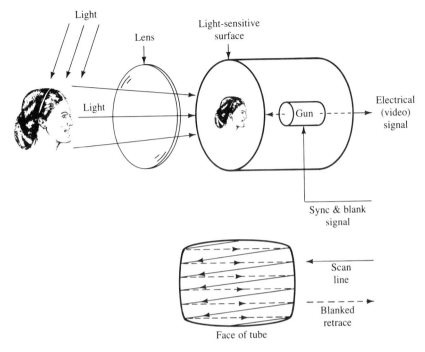

Figure 3-4 Picture conversion (black and white).

and green. These primaries must then be separately channeled, processed, transmitted to the receiver, and mixed properly to recreate the original scenic colors on a TV screen for the viewer (see Fig. 3-5).

Color Conversion.   Color conversion is accomplished in the same basic manner as black and white picture conversion, but with multiple conversions. The TV camera in the studio is aimed at a pictorial scene. The camera lens focuses the reflected light from the scene, projecting the exact light image of the scene into the camera's light filtering (dichroic filter) system. The light is separated into its red, blue, and green components, which are each projected onto a separate pickup tube. (The dichroic system acts much like a prism.) Each pickup tube is thus a separate channel for the image as displayed in its single color component. The output of each of the three pickup tubes is an electrical signal representation of the scene as seen through a single color filter, as it is scanned by the electron gun. Each of the three pickup tubes produces an electronic signal representation of the scene in a different primary color, and in exact scanning synchronization with each other. The resultant separate three outputs of the camera are a continuous flow of three synchronized electronic

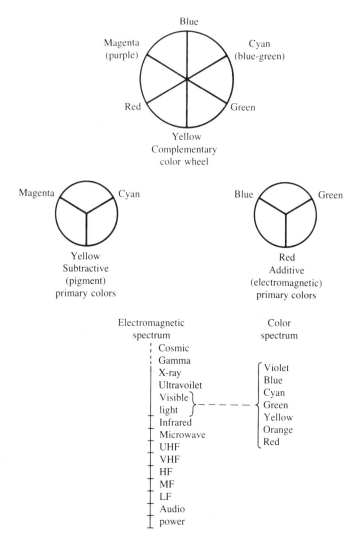

Figure 3-5 Primary colors.

signals, representing at any given moment an element of the pictorial scene separated into its red, blue, and green components (see Fig. 3-6).

Synchronization.   Before the system can work, all the parts must be synchronized together. Each of the three pickup tubes in the TV camera must be synchronized to scan exactly together. Since the picture tube in the TV receiver must be the reverse process of the TV pickup tube to display the picture properly, the receiver picture tube must be constantly in synchronization with the TV camera at the station. It becomes necessary then for the TV station to generate

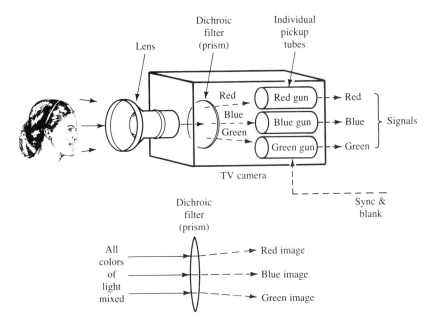

Figure 3-6   Color conversion.

synchronization (sync) signals to drive all the electron guns simultaneously, and to send this sync signal with the picture signal to the TV receiver to simultaneously drive its electron gun as the picture is being received. The sync generator of the TV station, therefore, sends a sync signal simultaneously to every electron gun in every camera, telling them exactly at what instant to start scanning scan-line number 1, then 2, etc., until the entire scene is scanned. Then it must signal all guns to reset back to the top of the scene to scan again. Additionally, so that the retrace of the scanning (the jumping back from the end of a line to the beginning of the next, or from the bottom of the picture back to the top) will not be visible, the sync generator also sends the guns a blanking signal to shut them off during this retrace action. All scanning guns then will be in exact step with each other every instant. This synchronization, or scanning, signal will be incorporated into the overall channel signal with the picture (video) signals from the camera and transmitter to the TV receiver (see Fig. 3-7).

Video Transmission.   The video transmitter is separate from the aural (audio) transmitter, and is a typical radio transmitter as explained by the original model. Since it operates at VHF or UHF frequencies, its physical plant facilities are visibly different from a transmitter in the AM or FM services, but its theoretical operation is essentially and basically the same. Its functions are to generate, modulate, and power-amplify an RF carrier signal, and to deliver it to an antenna for radiation.

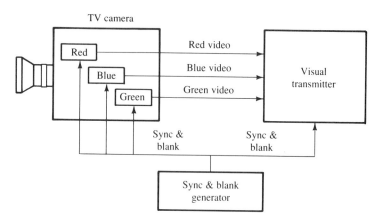

Figure 3-7   Video synchronization.

Monochrome Modulation.   The transmitter generates an RF carrier frequency in the VHF or UHF band. This carrier is then modulated with the video and sync/blanking signals. In order for this color transmission to be compatible with black and white TV sets (to display the color in black and white), a portion of each color signal is combined, with the sync/blank signals, and used to amplitude-modulate the main visual carrier frequency. Video frequencies or modulation produce a bandwidth of about 4 mHz; thus, normally this video information would create a sideband on each side of the carrier of 4 mHz, or a total bandwidth of 8 mHz. The FCC permits a total bandwidth of only 6 mHz for each TV channel, including the audio. To provide for this, the transmitter is designed to dispose of or eliminate most of the lower sideband. (Recall that sidebands are mirror images of each other, so no essential video intelligence will be lost.) However, since the lower sideband is not completely eliminated, but a vestige of it remains, this is called *vestigial sideband* amplitude modulation. When the black and white receiver processes the upper sideband, it will accept the mixed color signals as a single video signal to produce light intensities on the picture tube, or translate them into pictures of black, white, and shades of gray. The sync/blank signals contained in the video signal will control the picture tube's electron gun for proper picture reconstruction.

Color Modulation.   In addition to the modulation of the visual carrier by the combined color/sync/blank signals, a means is provided for the color signals to be conveyed individually as well, to provide color reconstitution in color TV sets. This is accomplished by the multiplexing of a subcarrier within the channel for separate color conveyance. A subcarrier frequency is selected that is far enough above the visual carrier that it will not interfere with the visual carrier's monochrome upper sideband. A portion of each individual color signal is used to amplitude-modulate the subcarrier, each at a different amplitude level so that they may be detected separately within the receiver. The upper and lower sidebands of this modulated subcarrier occupy the upper region of the visual channel width not required for the sidebands of the visual (main) carrier. All of the total video signals consisting of the modulated visual carrier (picture information) and the modulated subcarrier (color information) occupy approximately 5.5 mHz of the 6 mHz channel. The remaining approximately 0.5 mHz (500 kHz) remains to be occupied by the aural (audio) portion of the TV channel (a most generous allocation for audio).

The composite video signal consisting of the AM modulated carrier and sidebands of picture luminance with sync/blank information, and the AM modulated subcarrier of individual color information is power-amplified to the assigned power. It is then delivered to the antenna, where it will be joined with the signal from the separate aural transmitter. The combined visual and aural signals jointly make up the total television signal or channel (see Fig. 3-8).

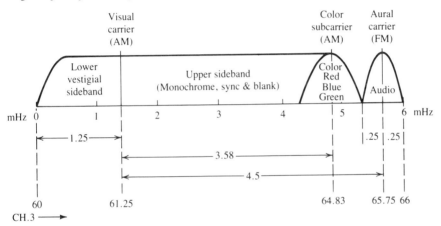

Figure 3-8 TV waveform structure (example: channel 3).

Waveform Structure.   Each TV channel is 6 mHz wide. The FCC requires that the visual carrier frequency be 1.25 mHz above the lower channel frequency limit, which leaves space for the vestigial lower sideband. The color subcarrier is required to be 3.58 mHz above the visual carrier. This spacing provides adequate space for the visual carrier upper sideband containing the picture (or luminance plus sync) information, and for the sidebands of the subcarrier (individual color information) without interfering with each other. All of this video information occupies all the channel space except for approximately 0.5 mHz. The aural transmitter carrier frequency is assigned the frequency 4.5 mHz above the visual carrier, which places it in the center of this aural space. This provides channel space of 0.5 mHz (500 kHz) for audio. Since audio modulation is limited to about 15 kHz, there is lots of empty audio space. (Look for future multiplexing for stereo, etc.)

Aural Transmission.   The aural (audio) transmitter is separate from the visual (video) transmitter. Its output will be combined with the visual transmitter output at the antenna. The aural transmitter essentially operates as a typical FM radio transmitter, but operating on a TV-assigned carrier frequency. The transmitter generates the proper VHF or UHF carrier wave, which is always 4.5 mHz above the visual carrier. The audio intelligence from studio microphones and other audio sources is sent to the modulator, where it is frequency-modulated onto the carrier. The FCC limits the range of permissible audio frequencies to 15 kHz (15,000 Hz). Since the reserved space for audio within the overall TV channel is about 0.5 mHz (500,000 Hz), it can be readily seen that the audio portion of the channel is grossly underutilized. This leaves plenty of empty space for multiplexing additional services. The modulated carrier with its sidebands of audio is power-amplified to the assigned power of the station. This aural signal is then delivered to the antenna for combining with the visual signal.

The Antenna.   Both the visual transmitter and the aural transmitter signals are applied to the common antenna through a diplexer unit. The essential purpose of the diplexer is to prevent the powerful signal of either the visual or aural transmitter from entering each other's transmitter to cause damage. The diplexer combines the signals from both the visual and aural transmitters for simultaneous propagation from the antenna, as an apparently composite TV signal representing all picture and sound information of the total 6-mHz-wide TV channel. In actuality, they are two separate but simultaneous transmissions to receivers that, when tuned to the channel, are broadly enough tuned to receive both as a single signal. The receiver will then process them separately. The antenna, like all antennas used for direct line-of-sight frequencies, is always mounted on a tall supporting tower at a high elevation in the area. Towers, of course, must always be marked and lighted for air navigation.

Polarization.   Standard television transmitting antennas are horizontally polarized. At VHF and UHF frequencies, the wavelengths permit full and half-wave antennas to be physically oriented in the horizontal plane. VHF-TV full wavelengths range from about 18 feet (channel 2) to about 4½ feet (channel 13), while UHF-TV wavelengths range from about 2 feet (channel 14) to about 1 foot (channel 69). This is the reason that rooftop TV receiving antennas are physically oriented in the horizontal plane. However, with the advent of portable and mobile TV sets that employ a vertical whip or telescoping antenna (horizontal antennas are physically impractical for these purposes), the FCC readily permits television stations to operate with circularly polarized antennas. This permits adequate reception by an antenna oriented in either plane.

Factors Determining Coverage.   At line-of-sight or direct-wave frequencies, the geographic area covered by the signal is not dependent solely on the power of the signals, as it is generally for ground wave communications. The extent of the coverage area at VHF and UHF frequencies is a combination of the factors of power, antenna height, and frequency. Power and antenna height are direct or positive factors, while frequency is an inverse or negative factor. The stronger the power of any signal, the farther it will go. The higher the antenna of any direct wave signal, the farther it will go. However, all other factors being equal, generally the higher the frequency, the less distance it will go with the same power and antenna height. A UHF signal requires more power and/or a higher antenna to travel as far as a VHF signal, one of the factors impeding parity of UHF with VHF stations.

Since television channels span such a wide range of VHF and UHF frequencies (54–806 mHz), and environmental conditions (topography, obstacles, etc.) vary so tremendously from area to area, the FCC could not establish a simple categorization of power assignments. Instead, it bases power assignments on channel assignment, antenna height, and location. The Commission, in its regulations, publishes charts providing guidance in this area. Suffice it to say that stations operating with lower antennas are permited higher power, and vice versa. UHF stations with lower towers (under 2000 feet) might operate with 5,000,000 watts, while a VHF station with a similar antenna might operate with 100,000 watts. As antenna height increases, these power assignments decrease. It must also be pointed out that the power of the visual and aural transmitters are considered and assigned separately. Depending upon other parameters, the ratio between visual and aural power is assigned to provide equal coverage of both the visual and aural signals. It is only reasonable that those who can see the picture should also be able to hear the sound, and vice versa. However, this is not always the case in fringe reception areas.

Propagation. The propagated wave from the TV transmitting antenna is a composite of a separate multiplexed amplitude-modulated visual transmitter and a simplexed FM aural transmitter combined together. This complex waveform occupies a channel 6 mHz wide within either the assigned VHF or UHF TV bands. Propagation at these frequencies is direct line of sight, limited to the horizon, which can be extended by antenna height. These frequencies tend to be subject to absorption, deflection, and blocking by obstacles. Since these effects are more pronounced with the higher channels, and since the UHF-TV band (470–806 mHz) is considerably higher than the VHF-TV band (54–216 mHz), the UHF channels suffer significantly greater deleterious effects—the higher the channel, the worse the effects. For these reasons, UHF channels require much greater power and antenna height (at tremendous expense) to be competitively received with VHF channels, and even then the effects cannot be totally overcome (yet another reason why UHF is inferior to VHF for TV reception).

Recall that amplitude modulation is subject to natural and man-made electrical interference, while frequency modulation tends to be immune from electrical interference. Additionally, FM receiver circuits provide an inherent "capture effect" of the FM signal, while received AM signals often suffer from co-channel signals creeping in on them (previously discussed in the AM and FM sections). For these reasons, the received sound portion of the TV channel is generally stable, clean, and clear, while the picture portion is sometimes subject to drift (breakup), co-channel interference (ghosts), and low signal-to-noise ratio ("snow"). In short, the FM sound is generally better and more reliable than the AM picture.

Ghosts. A word should be said about *ghosts* on the TV screen. There are two types of ghosts. One type is visible as secondary gray, transparent, and faint moving images within the otherwise acceptable picture. However, the gray transparent images have no relationship to, or are independent from, the primary picture. These ghosts are caused by co-channel interference, the picture from another but more distant station operating on the same channel. Such ghosts may be noticed by viewers in the fringe area of two overlapping TV stations on the same channel, where viewers see the stronger signal with the weaker signal in the background. The other type of ghosts are secondary double images, or sometimes triple images, within the picture. This causes the appearance of everything in the picture's having a reflection, shadow, or a second slightly offset image, or being out of focus. These ghosts are caused by the TV set's receiving two signals from the same station—one direct and one reflected (from a skyscraper, mountain, etc.). Since the reflected wave is the same signal, but arrives at the receiver a microfraction of an instant later, it is displayed on the TV screen correspondingly later, creating a shadow or ghost effect of the direct signal. In both ghosting situations, the audio is generally not affected, since the FM signal is stable, as described earlier (see Fig. 3-9).

Reception

Receiver Antennas. Fixed TV receiving antennas (such as those on houses) are horizontally oriented, since standard TV transmitting antennas are usually horizontally polarized. The higher they can be mounted, the stronger and more distant the signal they will generally receive as direct waves from TV stations. Ideally, the receiver would have a separate receiving antenna for each receivable station, and each would be a horizontal element as long as the equivalent wavelength of the signal received. The impracticality of multiple receiving antennas for each TV station resulted in the design of a common-type receiving antenna for all channels. This is an array of horizontal elements, connected together, and mounted on a common frame. Each element is physically approximately the wavelength or half-wavelength of the center frequency of a group of channels. Therefore, one element might be "cut" to channel 3 and receive channels 2, 3, and 4. Another might be cut to receive channels 5 and 6. Another, channels 7 through 10. Another, channels 10 through 13. Thus, perhaps four elements would receive the entire VHF TV band

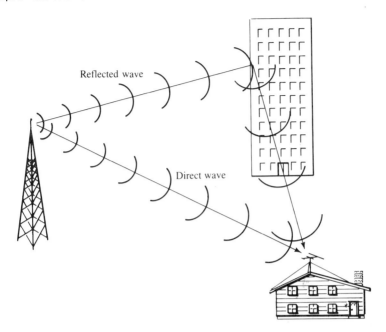

Figure 3-9 Reflective ghosting (multiple images).

adequately well if oriented toward the weakest station or to an average direction of all local stations.

UHF-TV channels are very much higher frequencies than VHF. Therefore, much smaller antennas are required, or antennas with greater receiving ability for those particular frequencies. Designs of the "bow tie" type have been found reasonably adequate to receive the UHF channels in a local area. In areas where UHF stations are few and distant, a separate parabolic reflector ("dish") antenna might be used for receiving a single UHF station.

Regardless of which type of antenna is used, reception will be greatly improved by aiming the antenna directly at the TV station. In professional applications, this generally means a separate antenna cut and aimed for each station received. In home-type situations, this usually means a compromise of a common array-type antenna aimed for optimum acceptable reception of all receivable stations in the area (see Fig. 3-10).

(a)   (b)   (c)

Figure 3-10 Types of TV receiving antennas. (a) VHF multichannel antenna; (b) UHF multichannel "bow tie" antenna; (c) UHF single-channel parabolic dish antenna.

Receiver Tuning.   The standard TV set is equipped with detent (or click-stop) tuning so that it is always tuned exactly to the center of the desired channel. This insures that the broadly tuned receiver will always receive the full 6 mHz bandwidth of the selected channel, making tuning simple. (Some older and portable sets do not have this feature, but have more difficult continuous tuning like most table model radios.) Once tuned to the selected channel, it is automatically set to receive the full channel width of picture, color, and sound information. The tuning section of the receiver, like a gatekeeper, permits the selected channel signal to proceed from the antenna into the processing circuitry. Within the receiver the visual signal and the aural signals are separated for demodulation and processing individually.

Receiver Signal Processing.   The visual signal is sent through the receiver's picture channel, which demodulates the visual carrier wave, separating the sideband information. This contains the image luminance information (the combined red, green, and blue images in their proper proportions), and sync/blanking information. (Black and white sets do not have the circuitry to demodulate the color subcarrier, and therefore the separate color signals are not used.) The image luminance information is sent to the TV picture tube through a video channel and the sync and blank information is sent to the picture tube through a sync channel (see Fig. 3-11).

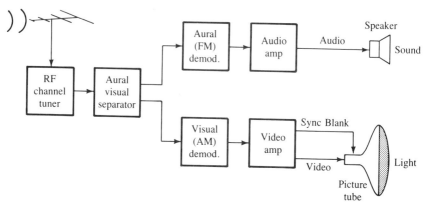

Figure 3-11 TV receiver block diagram.

Image Reconstruction.   The TV picture tube is constructed similarly to the studio camera tube, but operates in reverse process. It contains an electron gun that emits a fine beam of electrons, spraying the inside of the face of the tube. The inside face is coated with a phosphorescent coating that glows white when struck by the electron beam. When the TV set is turned on, but no signal is being received, the electron gun is spraying a maximum beam, but randomly. This makes the face of the picture tube glow white, but with a mottled (or tweed) appearance. When a sync signal is being received with no video, the electron gun is controlled in a steady sequential scanning pattern, which makes the face of the picture tube appear a solid even white color (called the *raster*, rhymes with master).

As the picture signal is applied to the electron gun, the signal controls the gun like a valve. When the signal is weaker, the gun sprays harder, making the screen glow whiter. As the signal grows stronger, the gun sprays less hard, making the screen grayer. When the signal is strongest, the gun stops spraying and the screen is black. Therefore, while the sync signal aims the gun in a continuous scanning process in exact sync with the camera tube, and the blank signal shuts the gun off during retrace, the picture signal causes the tube to reproduce the exact picture coming from the camera—but in black, white, and shades of gray. (This will not be a negative image of the camera signal, because the camera signal is inverted during the transmission process, resulting in the picture tube's creating a positive image) (see Fig. 3-12).

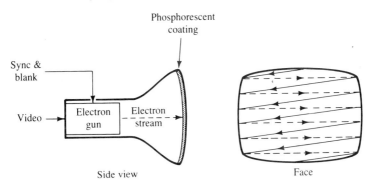

Figure 3-12   Image reconstruction.

Color TV Sets.   Color TV sets operate similarly to black and white TV sets as far as the luminance (black and white) image of the picture and the audio is concerned. Additionally, however, circuitry for color processing as well as a color picture tube are added. The TV set demodulates the color subcarrier and then separates the three primary color signals. These three separate color signals are then applied to separate electron guns in the color picture tube to recreate the originals through color mixing. The sync and blank signals control the scanning of all three guns to operate in unison (see Fig. 3-13).

Color Recreation.   Color TV sets are generally of the three-gun picture tube type (although there are others). The tube is similar to the picture tube in a black and white set, but more complex. The color tube contains three electron guns—one for each primary color. Additionally, the inside face of the tube is coated with tiny triads, or clusters, of color phosphors. Each triad consists of

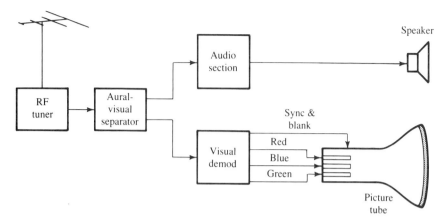

Figure 3-13   Color TV set block diagram.

three dots of different phosphors. When the phosphors are struck by an electron beam, one glows red, one blue, and one green. There are about 250,000 triads, each consisting of the same pattern of three color phosphors, or about 750,000 color dots arranged in triad patterns uniformly over the surface of the tube face. Between the guns and the face is a metal shadow mask perforated with about 250,000 tiny holes—one per triad.

The placement of the guns and shadow mask relative to the triad on the tube face is such that all three guns fire a stream of electrons through the same hole. The gun activated by the red signal will strike the red phosphors in each triad, while the blue gun strikes the blue phosphors, and the green gun strikes the green phosphors. If the strengths of the three electron beams are equal, the triad glows white from the mixture. If the beams are of different strengths, the triad will glow the appropriate resultant color from the color mixture. If no beam strikes the triad, it remains unlit, or black. Thus, the relative mixture of the red, blue, and green signal strengths determines the color the triad will glow.

The electron guns are scanned together, each aiming through the same mask hole at the same time, and therefore each is aimed at its appropriate color phosphor of each triad as it scans the face of the tube. The individual color signals vary the strength of the electron beams as they scan in unison, controlling the color mixture of each triad. The triads recreate the color image of the original pictorial viewed by the camera tube, while the persistence of the phosphorescence and of human vision perceive the glowing dots of various colors as a complete color picture (see Fig. 3-14).

TV Sound.   In all TV sets the aural or sound information is processed precisely as in an ordinary FM radio receiver. After the aural carrier is separated from the visual carrier, it is demodulated and processed through audio amplifiers. It is then applied to a standard radio speaker that converts the audio electrical

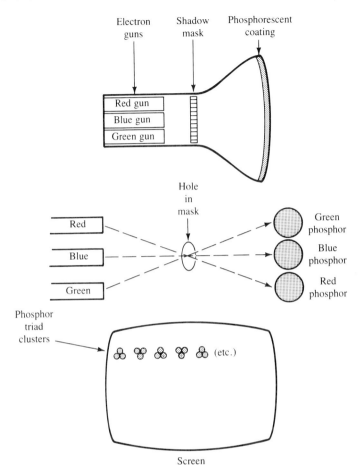

Figure 3-14 Color recreation.

signals back into their original corresponding sounds. Speakers are constructed to operate essentially like microphones in reverse, converting audio frequencies into acoustical energy, or sound.

Summary. The television station consists of a visual transmitter and an aural transmitter with a common antenna. Television cameras pick up light images and convert them into electrical video signals. The station synchronizing generator synchronizes all cameras together and also combines this sync signal with the video signal to ultimately synchronize the TV receiver with the station equipment. The visual transmitter generates an RF visual carrier, which is AM-modulated with the video and sync signals. It is then amplified and applied to the transmitting antenna. Simultaneously, microphones are picking up the associated sound of the scene, converting it into electrical audio signals. The aural transmitter generates an RF aural carrier that is FM-modulated with the audio, and it is then amplified and applied to the common transmitting antenna. Both carriers are separated only far enough apart in frequency so as not to interfere with each other, but are close enough to be received simultaneously by the receivers as a single channel signal. The broadly tuned receivers accept both carriers as one channel, separate them, and process them through separate AM and FM receiver circuits. The video output of the visual section is applied to the TV picture tube, which reconstructs the original image. The audio output of the aural section is applied to the speaker, which reconverts the accompanying sound.

TV TRANSLATOR

The Need.   The need exists for a translator service in television broadcasting as it does for the previously discussed FM translator. The television table of assignments, authorizing specific communities' committed TV channels, leaves discrepancies and "holes" in the intended national coverage plan. Many smaller communities end up with no television service at all, or are denied an educational or specialty station. To help correct some of these discrepancies and deficiencies, the FCC authorizes television stations in some instances to employ translators to extend their service to deprived communities. The FCC authorized translator service in 1956. In 1985, there were approximately 4800 TV translator stations in operation, with nearly 500 more authorized for construction.

The Technology.   The TV translator is merely a standard television broadcast transmitter that is authorized to extend the service area of its parent station. The translator is located in an area where the signal of the parent station is not sufficient to provide adequate service to the residents. It receives the signal from the distant parent station (usually off the air at a desirable vantage point) and rebroadcasts that same programming simultaneously on a different standard TV channel at low power. The translator is normally an automatic, unmanned facility that is not permitted to originate its own programming (however, see LPTV for exceptions). Since the translator employs the same technology and must adhere to the same technical regulations as standard broadcast TV transmitters, it is merely a variant application of standard technology rather than a different technology. It is merely a low-power rebroadcasting service. Since it is generally employed to extend the service area of a parent TV broadcast station into an adjacent area (or near community), the low power and different channel insure that no co-channel interference will occur (see Fig. 3-15).

Typical Scenario.   A typical scenario for a TV translator application might be as follows: A large city enjoys a full complement of both commercial

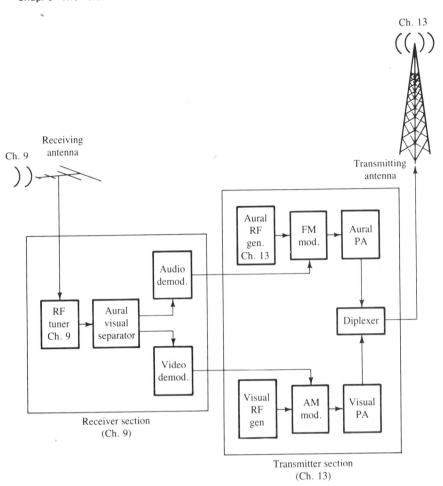

Figure 3-15 TV translator block diagram (example: channel 9 to channel 13).

and educational television stations. A hundred miles away is a rural town that is home to a university, small medical center, and two commercial television stations. Although the town is considered a cultural, educational, and medical center, its residents do not receive a single educational/cultural television station signal. The residents determine that the signal of one of the distant city's educational TV stations is receivable on top of a tower located 20 miles away. They take the initiative to gain rebroadcast rights from the TV station, petition the FCC for authorization, establish a community organization to fund the operation, and construct a translator station at the tower site. The translator receives the weak signal from channel 9 in the city, demodulates it, amplifies the video and audio signals, uses them to modulate the translator transmitter, and rebroadcasts the program simultaneously to the town on channel 13.

Summary. The TV translator is a device to extend the coverage of another originating station to an area outside its normal coverage area. Located in an area where it can receive the weak, unserviceable signal from the parent station, the translator receives the original signal, converts it to a different channel, and rebroadcasts it at a low power. Translators are authorized by the FCC in specific situations. The three distinguishing factors of a translator station are that they rebroadcast a signal from another station (they are generally not permitted to originate programming themselves, but see the LPTV section), operate at a low power, and rebroadcast on a channel different from the parent transmitter. They consist, therefore, essentially of a TV receiver that modulates a TV transmitter. Generally, TV translators are automatically controlled, unmanned stations. Since translators are essentially standard broadcast television transmitters, they do not constitute a different technology but merely a variant application of standard broadcast technology. As such, they must adhere to the same general technical regulations while extending the coverage of the parent station.

LPTV (LOW-POWER TELEVISION)

Overview. Low-power television (LPTV) is not a new technology. It is merely a logical extension of television translators which, by the magnitude of its potential, inaugurates a new broadcast service. Television translators have been in service since 1956 as low-power extensions of full-service TV stations, but they were precluded from originating programming themselves. In 1982, the FCC in effect lifted this restriction, encouraged translators to originate their own local programming, and opened the floodgates for innumerable new applications for additional low-power TV stations.

Development. Television translators are low-power TV stations that function merely to extend the range of a full-power TV station, and are not normally authorized to originate programming. However, there were exceptions where the FCC waivered the rule and authorized program origination; usually by video cassette and subcription TV service (see the next section on STV). These instances illustrated the viability of a low-power TV service. This, then, is the essence of LPTV. The FCC opened inquiry procedures to determine the need for and practicality of establishing a low-power television service. The results indicated a tremendous potential and demand. The Commission initiated rule-making proceedings to establish the service, and promptly received 7000 applications. The LPTV service was authorized in March, 1982, but the problem of processing the avalanche of applications resulted in a freeze, and necessitated subsequent major revision of procedures for the award of licenses. Although there are presently about 275 LPTVs in operation and another 210 authorized for construction, the number of pending applications is staggering.

The Need. The Low-Power Television Service is seen as a means to contribute some relief to several discrepancies in the national scheme of television service. The table of assignments for full-power TV stations leaves "holes" in the national coverage; some communities are not receiving television service due to insufficient coverage. Also, although some communities have channels assigned, full-power stations are economically impractical due to their tremendous costs. Translator operators and communities with translators are increasingly applying pressure on the FCC for permission to originate programming. Additional full-power stations cannot be assigned to many communities demanding local service, because the TV broadcast spectrum cannot contain more full-power stations without interference. Full-power stations discourage minority ownership because of their limited number and nonavailability to either build or buy, and because of their high cost. Service to rural areas by full-power stations is discouraged by economic realities and is limited to spillover from city service. Full-power television service is essentially owned by a few large organizations and serves general audiences with national programming of mass appeal, leaving smaller localized audiences wanting. TV localism is disappearing. LPTV is seen as some relief for all of these problems.

The Concept. Low-power television is envisioned as a means to restore localism in TV, to provide media ownership opportunities for minorities, to provide television service to any community without disrupting the structure of full-power service, to increase program diversity, to make efficient use of the TV spectrum, and to provide a plethora of other benefits. Since such a service has tremendous beneficial potential, but its viability is unknown, the FCC decided that LPTV must be given every opportunity to thrive. Consequently, although it is relegated to secondary status, it enjoys a tremendous degree of unregulation compared to full-service TV. As a secondary service, LPTV stations must not interfere with full-power stations. No LPTV applications will be approved that might interfere with a full-power station. Additionally, when both types of stations coexist, the LPTV must respond in any necessary manner to prevent interference resulting even from a later modification of the full-power station.

On the other hand, LPTV enjoys many benefits of nonregulation not enjoyed by any of the other services. Any entrepreneur can apply for an LPTV station for any community on any channel not already taken in that community. There are no prescribed distance separations or table of assignments. The applicant merely must show that the LPTV station would cause no interference to existing stations or allocated channels. There are no ownership restrictions on the number of stations owned. License application requirements and applicant qualifications are minimal. Processing procedures for LPTV applications have been streamlined. Applications for rural markets are given priority. The applications of minorities and women receive special consideration. Programming controls or requirements are almost nil. LPTV is designed to provide opportunities for new entrants into the television broadcast industry at a low cost, and in an environment conducive to success. However, although the FCC created an environment for success, it does not guarantee it; the (unknown) marketplace prevails.

The Technology. The technology of LPTV is the technology of the translator, which is the technology of standard television broadcasting on a low-power level. Therefore, LPTV stations are required to abide by the general technical regulations of full-power stations, but with many specific exemptions and reduced technical standards. Present translator stations can upgrade to LPTV status merely by notifying the FCC and commencing program orientation. New applicants can apply either for translators with the intention of subsequent upgrading, or can apply directly for LPTV licenses. The transmitter and antenna must be typically type-accepted equipment, operating on a standard TV channel (VHF or UHF). The assigned power for VHF LPTVs will normally be 10 watts for any channel not previously assigned to the community under the table of assignments, and will be limited to 100 watts under any circumstances. UHF LPTVs are limited to 1000 watts of power. Circularly polarized antennas are permissible. The stations can establish the appropriate program origination facilities for its purpose and marketplace (studio, network affiliation, videotape facilities, etc.). The propagation characteristics typical of the channel frequency and power will apply, will dictate the physical location and configuration of the antenna, and will determine the coverage area.

Summary. LPTV is merely a logical extension of the translator service. However, rather than extending the programming of another station, it employs standard (but low-power) television technology to originate and broadcast its own programming to a very limited community. In essence, an LPTV station is a miniature television station, so to speak. It is seen as a means to provide many small communities, especially in rural areas, with local television service and programming that would not otherwise have it. It also provides a means of low-cost entry into the television industry for minorities, and provides a source of diversified programming to specialized audiences. To insure that LPTV does not interfere with normal full-service television, it has been made a secondary service, subservient to the operations of full-power stations. However, to create an environment to encourage LPTV to succeed, the FCC has exempted it from many of the licensing, operational, and technical requirements of standard television broadcasting. The future of LPTV as a service depends upon the marketplace survivability of the individual stations.

STV (SUBSCRIPTION TELEVISION)

STV/PTV. Subscription television (STV) is often confused with pay television (PTV), which is understandable, since they both deliver premium television programming to subscribers who pay for the service. The primary difference between the two services, however, is in the delivery system. It has become standard within the industry that the term STV will apply to subscription television programming delivered to subscribers by over-the-air broadcast delivery, while the same type of service delivered to subscribers by cable TV system will be referred to as PTV (or pay cable). STV is subscription broadcasting, while PTV is subscription cable.

STV Concept.   The concept of the STV station is that of a standard broadcast television station that broadcasts premium TV programming (commercial-free first-run movies, live sporting events, night club performances, etc.) to the general public. However, the programming is *scrambled* (encoded, or encrypted) so that only paying subscribers can enjoy it. The monthly subscription fee entitles the subscriber to lease or buy a decoder unit that connects to his or her TV set and unscrambles (decodes) the received STV signal, restoring it to a normal program signal. Viewers who tune in the channel but do not have the proper decoder unit see only a confusion of unintelligible images on the screen and hear usually either nothing or recorded music. Some STV stations have, however, left the sound portion of the scrambled program intact, hoping that nonsubscribers will find the program sound so interesting and alluring that they will be enticed to subscribe to see the pictures as well.

Historical Perspective.   In the 1950s and 1960s, the FCC permitted experimentation with STV operations. Only a few stations operated during this period. As with every new medium, the press glorified the potential of STV, but it never lived up to those predictions. Nevertheless, entrepreneurs kept up the pressure on the FCC to approve STV service. In 1968, the FCC authorized regular STV stations. However, in strict comprehensive rules, the Commission in its usual fashion protected commercial broadcasting from this new service that could siphon programs and revenue away from it. In addition to requiring that STV stations conform to standard broadcast regulations and technical standards, the FCC imposed the following restrictions on STV stations:

1. An STV station could operate only in a community where there were already four other commercial TV stations.
2. There could be only one STV station in a market.
3. STV stations were required to broadcast at least 28 hours of "free" (nonscrambled) programming per week.
4. STV stations could not broadcast films more than two years old nor the sporting events of any team whose games were broadcast on commercial TV within the previous two years.

The rules were certainly not designed to promote the development of STV, and there were no regular STV operations during the next ten years.

Regulatory Perspective.   In 1977–1978, the FCC, in the process of generally deregulating broadcasting, eased many of the STV rules. Two stations went on the air, and the climate for STV development was friendlier. By 1981 there were 19 operating stations serving 864,000 subscribers, and 30 more stations on the drawing boards. A year later, STV service consisted of 27 stations in 18 markets serving 1,300,000 subscribers. The FCC, responding to both a general deregulatory frenzy in government and the success of STV stations, in 1982 agreed that STV should be permitted to develop fully within the marketplace. Between 1982 and 1983, the Commission nearly eliminated all of the restrictive rules of 1968. It eliminated the one-per-market and five-station-market rules, the 28 hours of free programming, and the prohibition on the sale of decoders. It also relaxed technical standards and reduced application requirements for STV, and permitted any TV broadcast station to operate an STV service. STV has been turned loose in the marketplace.

Economic Perspective.   STV has not enjoyed tremendous success in the past, and its future looks questionable. In the past, it generally broadcast special programming appealing to a narrow audience. Many stations programmed to specific cultural, language, or ethnic audiences, hoping to gain subscriber support to keep the unique programming on the air in the community. Local limited audiences, regardless of the intensity of their interest, did not provide an adequate subscriber base to finance operations. There was not enough mass appeal in the narrow-interest programming to attract a large general audience. As a result, most STV stations barely hung on, or quit. Presently, most STV stations are programming premium fare that appeals to a large general audience to acquire a large subscriber base. This works well enough for nighttime programming, but the subscriber base is not sufficient for daytime programming when the audience is small. Additionally, in communities where cable TV provides PTV services, STV competes at a disadvantage. Cable can provide several channels of PTV at less cost than STV stations can provide a single channel. STV is limited to a single channel, which is considerably more expensive to deliver. The future of STV faces tough competition from cable, SMATV (Satellite Master Antenna Television), VCRs (video cassette recorders), and other new technologies.

Operational Overview.   The present-day model of typical STV operations is a standard independent (nonnetwork affiliated) television broadcast station providing normal free commercial programming during the day and STV scrambled programming at night. The station is usually (but not necessarily) a UHF independent station. This is true for two good reasons: Applications for new stations usually must be for UHF because the VHF allocations in most communities have been taken long ago, and existing stations that choose to provide STV service are those independent UHF stations that are losing money commercially (VHF stations do not normally lose money) in normal operations. Although the STV station might have a sufficient subscriber base for nighttime programming, it generally cannot afford to provide subscriber-supported daytime programming when that audience is too small to economically justify it. The station therefore usually operates during the day as a normal commercial broadcast station to generate additional revenues from commercial advertising, and switches to scrambled premium programming for subscribers at night. This optimizes the economic base of the station.

Typical Format.   A typical format for a STV station emerges. The UHF independent station operates during the day as a normal broadcast station. It might affiliate with a specialty network such as a religious network (PTL, CBN, and the like), financial services (Financial News Network, etc.), or foreign language network (Spanish International Network—SIN). It might otherwise operate as a typical independent, buying old reruns and movies, and producing its own local shows. It will, however, sell commercial advertising for its economic base. Sometime during early evening (between six and eight o'clock) the commercial operation will sign off, and the station will program for the rest of the night in scrambled mode, delivering premium commercial-free programming to its subscribers who possess the decoders. The programming generally will be first-run movies, live championship sporting events, live concerts and night club acts, and similar fare. Additionally, the STV operation may affiliate with entertainment networks such as HBO, Showtime, The Playboy Channel, etc., to provide unique programming. Some stations offer late-night adult sex movies, which might be specially scrambled (complex or super scrambling) to require an additional subscription fee for this additional service.

STV Technology.   The technology of the basic STV station, or delivery system, is exactly that of the typical television full-service broadcast station. The special technology involved is the means of protecting the security of the programming from nonsubscribers and "pirates." In short, STV technology consists of encoder-decoder (scrambling/descrambling) or security system technology. This security system technology is relatively new, is very sophisticated, and is in a constant state of flux. Shortly after a manufacturer markets a security system, a copied version of his descrambler appears on the bootleg market and program piracy begins. The manufacturers design a more sophisticated system to thwart the pirates, and the bootleggers eventually produce a box to beat that system; so it goes. The war never ends. This constant battle for security produces a wide array of various types of encoders and decoders for an ever-changing market. This discussion must be limited, therefore, to a general treatise on the basic technique of program security—to which there are many variations.

Visual Scrambling. The STV transmitter is a typical TV broadcast transmitter described in earlier sections. It consists of separate visual and aural transmitters feeding a common antenna. The visual transmitter generates the RF visual carrier, modulates it with the video and sync information, power-amplifies this composite visual signal, and applies it to the antenna. However, the transmitter employs an additional stage of processing when operating in the STV mode. This stage, the encoder, can operate in somewhat different ways in different security systems. The encoder can modulate the transmitted sync signal with a particular frequency or coded pulses so that on a TV set the picture appears completely out of sync, or totally broken up beyond recognition. An encoder can modulate the transmitted video signal similarly so that the picture content appears on a TV set to be intolerably "garbaged up," or the entire normal visual TV signal might be multiplexed totally to shift it to a different channel. Any of these processes might be used simultaneously, or variations of them might be used. In any event, the encoder in the transmitter adds extra modulation or multiplexing of the visual signal that standard TV sets are incapable of processing, or destroys or inverts the picture sync or other information, rendering the picture undecipherable. Any of these methods destroys normal picture reception of that particular channel. A subscriber who possesses a decoder box for that system connects it between his receiving antenna and TV set. As the encoded signal passes through the decoder on the way to the TV set, its circuitry provides the precise demodulation and/or demultiplexing required to restore the signal to normal as it enters the TV set to be processed normally. The decoder unit is switched on only when the viewer tunes in the STV channel. For all other channels the decoder is switched off to prevent it from affecting them, and the decoder is effectively by-passed (see Fig. 3-16).

Sound Security. The sound portion of the TV signal is sometimes not distorted, but is presented to the nonsubscriber intact. The theory is that when viewers tune in the STV channel and hear an exciting program but cannot see what is happening, they will be sufficiently frustrated and motivated to subscribe to the service to enjoy this exciting service. In other security systems, the sound is either eliminated completely or is substituted by a different and unassociated sound program, such as recorded music or a local radio station. Understandably, the sound is usually not "garbaged" like the video, for that would be translated as a cacaphony of noise in the viewer's living room whenever he or she tuned past that channel, causing the STV operator great public relations problems.

Audio Scrambling. The aural transmitter of the STV station operates like a typical FM radio transmitter, as described previously. The transmitter generates an RF carrier which is modulated by the program audio; the aural signal is power-amplified and applied to the common transmitting antenna. In

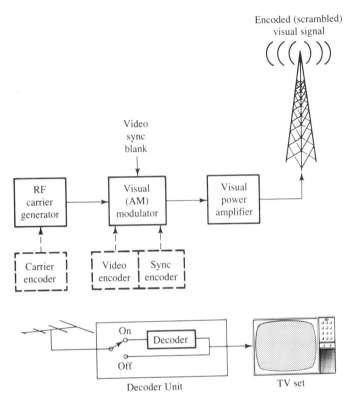

Figure 3-16 (a) Visual encoding options; (b) receiver decoder.

STV systems which alter the sound, the purpose is to prevent nonsubscribers from enjoying the actual sound of the program. Probably the simplest way would be to modulate the carrier a second time with a second, unpleasant, audio signal accompanying the program audio. However, since this unpleasant sound could cause consternation to nonsubscribers when tuning past the STV channel, this is not a good practice for STV operators. An alternative is to eliminate the sound completely from nonsubscribers' sets. To do this, the transmitter must encode the audio with a code of pulses that will activate the subscriber's decoder to permit the aural signal to pass into the receiver, or to multiplex the aural signal with a frequency that will shift it beyond the tuning capability of the TV set, but will be demodulated (or shifted back) by the subscriber's decoder. Either of these techniques will eliminate the program sound from the nonsubscriber's set.

Audio Substitution.   An added sophistication is to replace the deleted program sound with recorded music or audio from a local radio station. This can be accomplished by modulating the multiplexing frequency above with recorded music or audio from a radio station. The TV without a decoder will receive as the aural signal the modulated multiplexed carrier as substitute for the modulated aural carrier. In sets with decoders, the decoders will demultiplex the signal, shifting the aural carrier back to its original place in the channel, but shifting the multiplexing carrier beyond tuning range of the channel selector. This dual carrier multiplexing arrangement is a means merely to carry two programs simultaneously, which will be shifted into or out of the TV set's STV channel bandwidth.

Future Security Needs. These are merely some of the presently possible general techniques to accomplish STV program security. There are other applications and innovations, and there will be more diverse and complicated STV security technologies in the future. However, they must all generally be based upon similar principles and applications to accomplish the same purposes. Program security is a dynamic and burgeoning industry within itself.

Summary. Subscription television (STV) is merely the broadcasting of premium commercial-free programming with a means of requiring those who view it to pay for it. Employing standard broadcast television technology, STV incorporates an electronic means of protecting the security of the programming from nonsubscribers. This security system consists of scrambling the television signal at the transmitter and descrambling it by means of a decoder at the receiver. The technology of the program security systems is in a constant state of flux, and constitutes a dynamic and burgeoning industry. Manufacturers wage a constant and escalating war of development to keep ahead of the program pirates.

The typical STV station is an independent UHF broadcast station during the day, and an STV operation at night. The daytime operation consists usually of a typical independent station programming and/or affiliating with a specialty network (PTL, SIN, FNN, etc.) and supported by commercial advertising. At night the station goes into a scrambled mode and broadcasts premium commercial-free programming to subscribers provided with descramblers. STV programming consists generally of first-run movies, live special entertainment and sporting events, and cultural events. Additionally, the STV operation may affiliate with an entertainment pay-TV operation such as HBO, Showtime, The Playboy Channel, etc. Some stations program late-night adult sex movies, which are often scrambled with an additional security technique to require STV viewers to pay an additional premium for a converter capable of descrambling the "super" scrambled programming. And so it goes.

The future of STV operations is questionable. Stiff competition from pay cable, SMATV, VCRs, and other technologies puts the economic basis of STV on uncertain ground.

MTS (MULTICHANNEL TELEVISION SOUND)
TV STEREO
SAP (SECOND AUDIO PROGRAM CHANNEL)
PC (PROFESSIONAL CHANNEL)

The Need. With both the FM and AM radio services authorized to employ subcarriers for the purposes of broadcasting stereo and other nonbroadcast services, it was to be only a matter of time and technology before television would follow suit. In 1977, a TV broadcaster requested that the FCC permit TV aural subcarrier use for the audio cuing of electronic newsgathering teams in the field. The FCC responded by launching an official study of the possibility and practicality of TV aural subcarriers for a variety of uses, including: news-crew cuing, TV stereophonic sound, bilingual simultaneous programming, augmented audio for the blind, and other unforeseen uses. The response was so enthusiastic that in 1979 the FCC proposed to allow limited use of aural subcarriers for specified limited operational functions (newsroom cuing and coordination, etc.).

Industry Recommendation. In the meantime, a television trade association (Electronic Industries Association—EIA) formed a committee to conduct feasibility studies and develop technical standards for the FCC's consideration. EIA's recommendation included a stereo sound channel, a second audio program channel (SAP), and other multipurpose subcarrier channels. In December 1983, EIA's efforts culminated in the selection of one of three competing multichannel television sound (MTS) transmission systems. The industry-selected system, developed by Zenith, is referred to as the *BTSC system*, having been selected by the Broadcast Television Systems Committee of the EIA. This BTSC system was proposed to the FCC as the industry standard; however, all industry members were not in agreement with that system as the best standard.

A Quasi-Standard. The FCC was faced with a major decision. To not adopt a subcarrier standard for TV, and leave the decision to the marketplace would cause a repeat of the AM stereo fiasco and would retard the service. To establish a single standard to which there was not industry consensus would be to preclude independent development leading to more diversified and effective systems and services. To surmount this dilemma, the Commission decided not to decide, but chose instead a compromise from which it would receive the least intense criticism (and also the fewest accolades). It established the BTSC system as a protected system (thus, a quasi-standard) which others could follow, or not, at their option. Other manufacturers are free to develop their own TV aural subcarrier systems within the general parameters of TV signal requirements, but these other systems cannot interfere with the protected BTSC (Zenith) system. This insures that consumers buying TV sets with the BTSC stereo capability, and broadcasters transmitting the BTSC stereo signal will have their investments protected, while manufacturers are free to develop other systems to compete in the TV stereo marketplace.

Overview of the Technology.   There has been only one system (the BTSC system) of television aural subchannel utilization accepted and protected by the FCC, creating a protected quasi-standard. Although other manufacturers are free to develop competing systems, the technological principles involved will require them to be generally similar to the BTSC system, varying primarily in the subchannel carrier spacing, subchannel width, pilot signal, etc. Since the overall concept of any subcarrier system developed will be similar to the BTSC system, this discussion will be limited to that system, but will generally be applicable to all MTS systems.

The Potential.   Each TV channel occupies 6 mHz of frequency spectrum. Approximately 5.5 mHz of this is dedicated to the video signal, leaving approximately 0.5 mHz of frequency space for the aural signal. As has been discussed previously, the entire audio frequency spectrum consists of less than 20 kHz (20,000 Hz). The FCC arbitrarily limited the amount of audio for the TV aural signal to 15 kHz (15,000 Hz), which is amply adequate for high fidelity sound. Thus, since only 15 kHz of the 0.5 mHz (500 kHz) aural signal space is used by the TV program audio, simple mathematics reveals that about 485 kHz of aural space is unused. It is readily obvious that many more audio signals, or program services, could be carried simultaneously within that space. It is merely a matter of establishing modulated subcarriers within that channel space, spaced far enough apart to avoid interference with each other, to create independent aural subchannels. The modulation on each of these subchannels can be associated with or totally independent from the main TV aural channel programming. The technology is essentially the same as for FM radio SCA services (stereo and others); see Fig. 3-17.

The BTSC Services.   The BTSC system provides for three aural subchannel services in addition to the main aural program channel. These subchannels consist of a TV stereo subchannel, a second audio program subchannel (SAP), and a professional or operational subchannel (PC). When all subchannels are fully occupied (used), this permits a TV station to broadcast simultaneously monophonic sound, stereophonic sound, a second audio program either associated with the TV program (second language?) or independent from it (an independent radio program?), and private voice or data information for the station's own internal operations or for specific subscriber audiences.

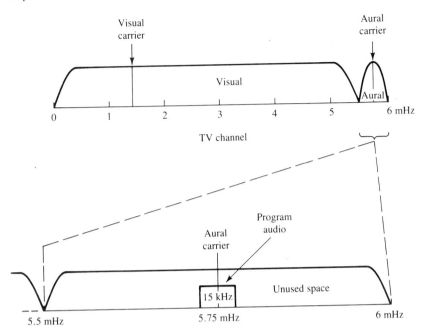

Figure 3-17   Aural channel space.

Creation of Subchannels.   A subchannel is created for each different aural subchannel (MTS) service in essentially the same way that FM stereo and SCA subchannels are created within the FM service. An unused frequency within the TV aural spectrum space is designated as the subcarrier for each subchannel service. These subcarriers must be spaced far enough from the main aural channel and from each other so that their modulated sidebands do not interfere with the others. Each subcarrier is modulated independently from the others, and this modulation can be in the form of FM or AM (or other types of modulation such as phase, pulse, etc.), depending upon the system design and intended service. Subchannels may also employ a pilot frequency (or tone) to accompany the subchannel signal to automatically activate necessary circuits, indicator lamps, or serve other functions within the receiver for proper reception of the subchannel signal. The following discussion describes generally the BTSC system operation.

The Main Aural Channel.   The main or aural program channel of all TV signals is a carrier frequency spaced at the 5.75 mHz point within the 6 mHz TV channel, or 5.75 mHz above the lower frequency limit of the TV channel. It is FM-modulated and is permitted a bandwidth of 15 kHz of audio. This aural channel carries all of the program audio in the present monophonic TV broadcasting systems, as in monophonic AM or FM broadcasting. If a TV station begins broadcasting a stereo signal, the main aural channel must still carry all of the sound for compatibility with existing monophonic TV sets, yet the main channel must act as the carrier for only one audio signal for stereo TV sets, the other audio signal (channel) being carried on a separate subcarrier. This is accomplished as in radio stereo broadcasting, where the station's original two distinct audio signals are carried by the same carrier, but each with a different phase (or other) relationship with the other. A monophonic TV set will not distinguish the difference in the phase relationship, and will process both audio signals as one through the common receiver audio section. A stereo TV set, however, will distinguish the difference and reproduce only one of the audio signals in the main channel, relying on a stereo subchannel to provide the other as a separate signal.

The Stereo Subchannel.

TV stations broadcasting in stereo will, in addition to the main channel modulation technique above, provide a subchannel for the second (stereo) audio signal. The stereo subchannel is created by injecting (or amplifying) another frequency within the aural space of the TV channel and AM-modulating it with the second audio signal. This subcarrier is located about 30 kHz above the main channel carrrier, to provide ample room for the sidebands without interference. It is permitted 15 kHz of bandwidth to match the audio fidelity of the main channel audio signal. The subcarrier is accompanied by a pilot frequency that automatically activates the TV set's stereo circuits that light the stereo signal indicator, extracts and reproduces only one audio signal from the main channel, and reproduces the second audio signal through the separate audio channel of the set. Thus, stereo sound compatibility has been achieved for both monophonic and stereophonic TV sets (see Fig. 3-18).

The Second Audio Program Channel (SAP).

The second audio program channel (SAP) (see Fig. 3-18) is established to provide the TV station with the capability of transmitting another audio program in addition to main channel audio. The most common example often cited is a foreign-language sound track for the TV program, which could be switched on in place of the normal program audio. The SAP is not, however, required to be associated with the TV program or the main aural channel. It can carry a completely separate audio program, much like a separate radio program. This service can be provided to the general public or can be operated as a separate commercial service to special subscribers. This subchannel, like any other, is created by injecting (or amplifying) another of the unused frequencies within the aural space of the TV channel and modulating it separately. The SAP subcarrier is spaced about 47 kHz above the stereo-assigned subcarrier (or 78 kHz above the main aural channel

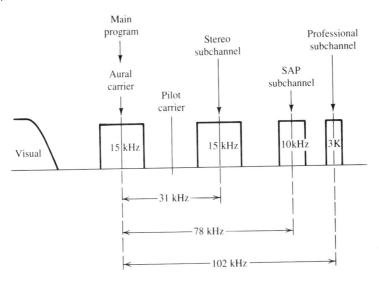

Figure 3-18 TV aural subchannels.

carrier) so that the sidebands will not interfere with each other. The SAP subchannel occupies a bandwidth of 10 kHz for FM modulation. This permits an audio program of adequate fidelity for most purposes (similar in quality to AM radio). The TV receiver requires a special audio circuit to receive the SAP subchannel. Also, small receiver units can be designed to receive the SAP audio subchannel much as a radio does, without the video capability.

The Professional Channel (PC). Provision has been made for a professional subchannel for operational uses by the TV station. This subchannel is intended primarily for the TV station to cue news crews in the field, communicate with personnel at remote station sites, control remote equipment, and other similar station-related activities. Another use is to provide information and data service to subscriber businesses. This subcarrier is spaced approximately 24 kHz above the SAP subcarrier, or 102 kHz above the main channel aural carrier (see Fig. 3-18). Since its use is designated for FM voice or data transmission, which requires less sideband space than music, it is permitted a bandwidth of only 3 kHz.

Summary. Since the aural allocation or space of the TV channel is not fully used by the program audio, ample space remains in which aural subcarriers can be employed to provide additional subchannel audio services. The television industry recommended to the FCC what is known as the BTSC system as a standard for TV aural subcarrier services. The FCC favored this system with protection from other manufacturers, but stopped short of precluding the development and implementation of other systems. The BTSC established the precedent services, however, which future systems will be prone to emulate—with differences. The BTSC system provides for three subchannel audio services in addition to the main program aural carrier. A stereo subcarrier provides stereophonic TV sound that is compatible with monophonic TV sets. A second audio program (SAP) subcarrier provides for another audio program channel that can broadcast a separate audio signal related to or independent from the main TV program. A third professional subchannel (PC) permits voice or data communications to field or remote units of the TV station, or acts as a service to other business subscribers. Although the BTSC systems established the precedent system, others may be developed and employed which differ in technical detail: spacing of subchannels, use of pilot signals, type of modulation, and other intricacies. Nevertheless, TV multichannel sound (MTS) is accomplished by the established general principles of multiplexing techniques.

the microwave (terrestrial) media

4

ITFS (INSTRUCTIONAL TELEVISION FIXED SERVICE)

Purpose. The Instructional Television Fixed Service (ITFS) was established essentially as a means whereby educational institutions could establish a private television distribution system between buildings, or intracampus. The purpose is to distribute television programming of an instructional or cultural nature from a central point to multiple classroom reception points. When not actually transmitting instructional/cultural programming to classrooms, the institution may transmit administrative information used in direct support of the academic function. This could include administrative information, faculty in-service training, professional development, safety instructions, and similar communications. Eligibility to be an ITFS licensee is limited to institutions or government organizations engaged in formal educational activities, or to other nonprofit organizations providing instructional material for these academic organizations.

Historical Perspective. In 1961, a public school system on Long Island received from the FCC permission to experiment with establishing its own private television system to distribute instructional TV programming from a central location to all of its outlying school buildings. The school experimented with the little-used 2-gHz microwave band, which was ideal for short-range, low-power, line-of-sight, private, and low-cost transmission. Subsequent demonstrations impressed the FCC chairman with the potential of private television service for educational institutions. In 1963, the FCC established the Instructional Television Fixed Service (ITFS). The following year the first two systems were operating at public school systems in New York and Ohio. Within three years the FCC had received more than 120 applications for more than 330 channels. In 1972, the FCC made an allocation of 28 channels within the 2500–2690 mHz (2 gHz) band, each wide enough to carry a standard television signal—6 mHz wide. It additionally authorized a paired return voice/data channel for each TV channel, but which was only 125 kHz wide. The 28 TV channels and their paired 28 voice/data return channels were divided into blocks of four paired channels. This would permit each institution to apply for and operate as many as four channels for a multichannel operation. Educators and government alike envisioned that ITFS would contribute significantly to education.

New Developments.   Actual utilization of ITFS did not live up to anticipation. By the early 1980s, many ITFS channels remained unused in many parts of the country, and it appeared that ITFS growth was unlikely to exhaust its supply of channels. Meanwhile, a new commercial service called Multipoint Distribution Service (MDS) was clamoring for more frequencies. MDS was a private microwave service that distributed pay television programming within a local area. The demand for MDS had outstripped channel availability, its growth potential was obvious, and there was a need to create a multichannel MDS (see next section on MDS). Thus, in 1983, the FCC took away eight of the ITFS channels and reallocated them to MDS. To soften the blow to ITFS, the FCC grandfathered the ITFS systems existing on the reallocated channels (permitted them to remain on channel, with protection from interference from MDS). Additionally, to promote better use of the ITFS channels, the FCC authorized ITFS stations to lease their unused capacity to other entities on a profit-making basis. In other words, a school district using an ITFS for daytime instructional use may now lease its nonused nighttime operation to a commercial entrepreneur for MDS or similar operation.

Present Status.   Unfortunately, like instructional radio and instructional television, ITFS did not really catch on. In spite of the high hopes, good intentions, and vigorous support of the educational community in general, that community was not able to harness ITFS for practical purposes to a significant degree. Perhaps due to lack of funds, lack of knowledge, professorial resistance, or any of the other reasons variously offered, the result is obvious: Institutions using ITFS are the rare exceptions rather than the rule. There are presently 250 operational systems presently licensed, with as little more than 100 construction permits for new stations.

Overview of the Technology.   Instructional Television Fixed Service (ITFS) is a private one-way system of distributing instructional television programs from a central point to multiple receiving points. It does provide for a return voice/data channel from each receiving site back to the central transmitting point. The service uses frequencies in the 2 gHz microwave band because they are suitable for short-range, low-power, line-of-sight, inexpensive communications. Additionally, since the general public normally has no equipment to receive microwave signals, the system is private. Each system is authorized to employ up to four separate channels (requiring a separate transmitter for each channel) with its paired return voice/data channel.

Overview of Operation.   In a single-channel system, the institution would install a microwave transmitter and antenna in a centrally located building. Each classroom building (and office building) designated to receive the TV programming would be equipped with a microwave antenna, a unit to change the microwave signal to a standard TV signal (a downconverter), and a standard TV receiver. A classroom building might be cabled throughout so that the received TV signal, after downconversion to a standard TV channel, could be distributed to standard TV sets located throughout the building (see Fig. 4-1).

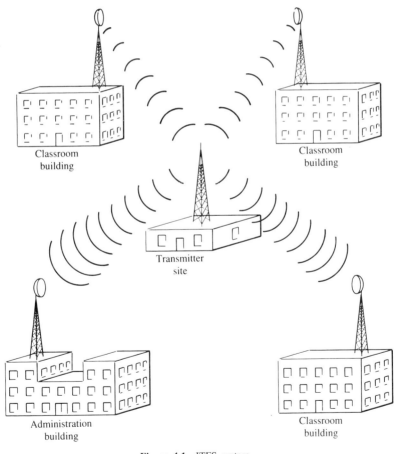

Figure 4-1 ITFS system.

The Transmitter. The transmitter of the ITFS system is technologically similar to a standard TV broadcast transmitter. However, because of the high frequencies (microwave) and low power (10 watts), the transmitter is much smaller. Both the visual and aural transmitters are usually contained within a single "box." A visual transmitter generates a microwave carrier frequency which is amplitude-modulated by a video signal from studio cameras or videocassette. An aural transmitter generates a microwave carrier which is frequency-modulated with the audio signal associated with the video. The modulated visual and aural carriers are power-amplified and fed to the common antenna, where they are radiated together as a single microwave television channel signal. The specifications for this channel must meet the same specifications as a broadcast TV channel, relative to the TV signal; essentially, only the carrier frequencies are different.

The Transmitting Antenna. The microwave signal is emitted from an antenna usually elevated on a tower or mast on top of the building. The FCC requests that directional antennas aimed toward the receiving sites be used whenever possible to increase efficiency and decrease interference with other signals. The antenna radiating element itself is very small, in the neighborhood of ½-inch long at microwave lengths. For directional antennas, this element is positioned in front of a reflector or parabolic dish to concentrate the radiated energy into a directional pattern or beam. The radiating element is permitted to be either horizontally or vertically polarized (oriented), whichever provides the best interference-free reception. Tower marking regulations apply for aircraft safety.

Coverage Factors. The coverage area of the signal depends on several factors: the propagation characteristics inherent in microwaves, power, antenna height, antenna directional characteristics, and obstacles in the environment. Microwave frequencies are highly line of sight, reflective, and absorptive. Therefore, the path of the radiated signal must be line of sight and reasonably clear of obstacles. The higher both the transmitter and receiver antennas are mounted, the greater the distance achieved, and probably the fewer the obstructions encountered. The more directional the radiated pattern can be to reach all receiver sites, the more strongly the signal will radiate to them. Nondirectional transmitting antennas are not as efficient, spreading the same amount of signal over a broader area and decreasing signal range. Considering all of these factors, the FCC requires a system to use no more power than required to accomplish adequate communications to its receiver sites. Transmitters are generally limited to 10 watts of power, unless a specific showing justifies a waiver. Coverage areas of 5 to 20 miles are typical. The Commission does permit the use of microwave translators to extend coverage, when justified.

Frequency Allocation. The FCC had originally allocated those frequencies between 2500 and 2690 mHz in the 2 gHz microwave band for ITFS operations. This provided 31 channels, each 6 mHz wide, for television carriage. These 31 channels were grouped into four-channel groups for multichannel operation. Since that time, in 1983, the FCC has given some of the ITFS channels to the rapidly growing MDS service, and requires ITFS to share some other frequencies with the Private Operational Fixed Microwave Service (OFS). Presently, therefore, ITFS enjoys the exclusive use of 16 channels from 2500 to 2596 mHz, and shares seven channels from 2644 to 2686 mHz with OFS. The eight channels from 2596 to 2644 mHz were given to MDS. Additionally, the 4 mHz from 2686 to 2690 mHz is divided up into the paired voice/data return channels, each 125 kHz wide (see Fig. 4-2).

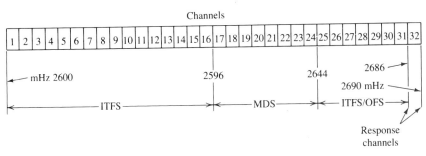

Figure 4-2   ITFS frequency allocation.

The Receiving Site. The microwave signal radiated from the transmitting antenna is a television signal being carried on a microwave carrier wave. The receiving site must therefore be equipped with a microwave receiving antenna, a means to convert the microwave carrier to a normal or standard TV channel, and a standard TV set with which to view the programs. Once the signal is converted to a standard TV channel, it can be distributed by cable throughout the building to various TV sets simultaneously. (Refer to the section on MATV.)

The Receiving Antenna. The signal is intercepted by a directional microwave dish or other receiving antenna aimed at the transmitter site. The dish, or reflector, gathers in maximum signal strength and focuses it on the receiving antenna element. The antenna element must be polarized in the same plane as the transmitting antenna for maximum efficiency. The maximized signal is then fed to the downconverter. The receiving antenna should be elevated as high as possible with a direct line of sight to the transmitting antenna to achieve the best reception (see Fig. 4-3).

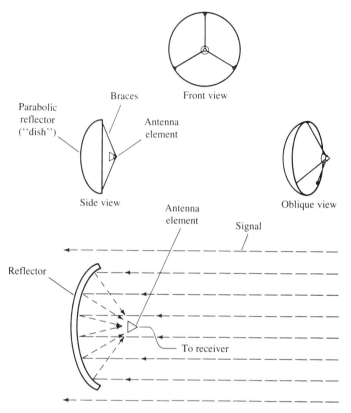

Figure 4-3 Parabolic reflector dish antenna.

The Downconverter.   The downconverter is generally mounted on the antenna mast or tower, as near to the antenna as possible to prevent signal loss. The function of the converter is to convert the microwave carrier frequency down to a standard broadcast TV channel. Recall the discussion in earlier chapters; when two frequencies are electronically mixed ("beat") together, the result is a frequency equal to the difference between the two. If one of the original frequencies was modulated, that modulation appears on that difference frequency. Therefore, the converter has circuitry within it which generates another frequency that is of a predetermined frequency that, when beat with the incoming microwave, will produce a difference frequency which is the same as a standard VHF TV channel. This difference carrier will contain the original modulation of the microwave signal, and can be tuned in by a standard TV set, just as though it had been originated as a standard TV broadcast signal. A simple downconverter can be employed to convert four microwave signals simultaneously to different TV channels (see Fig. 4-4).

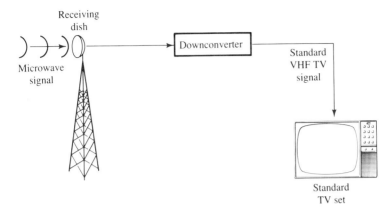

Figure 4-4   Downconversion.

The Receiver.   The downconverted signal has been changed to a standard TV broadcast signal. The converter is, of course, designed to convert the microwave signal to an unused TV channel in the area. This signal is sent to a standard TV set that tunes in the signal as a normal broadcast signal. In most institutional situations, however, the signal is first amplified and then distributed throughout the building on coaxial cable to many classroom and office outlets. Standard TV sets can then be plugged into any of the cable outlets and tuned in simultaneously. Of course, the program can be viewed when received, or it can be recorded on videotape for later playback (see Fig. 4-5).

Response Channels.   Each ITFS system is authorized a response channel paired with each ITFS channel assigned; thus, if a system operates the full complement of four channels, it is authorized to utilize the four paired response channels. Each receiver site is permitted to have a small microwave transmitter with which to beam response communications back to the ITFS transmitter site. Each of the multiple receiver sites for a single channel transmits on the same response frequency—sort of a party line arrangement. The response channel will carry only voice or data, but not video (since its bandwidth is only 125 kHz wide). The response transmitter must be operated by the same institution that operates the ITFS system, and it must communicate only to the ITFS origination site. It is required to use a highly directional antenna aimed at the ITFS station. Response transmitters are limited to 250 milliwatts (¼ watt) of power unless a waiver is granted; then they are limited to 2 watts of power.

Summary   ITFS is primarily authorized as a private distribution system for academic institutions to distribute instructional television programming from a central point to other of their academic buildings. The technology is

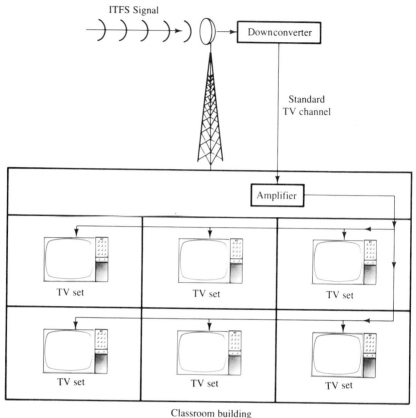

Figure 4-5   Typical ITFS receiver system.

typical of standard broadcast stations, except that the carrier frequencies are microwave frequencies. The television signal carried by the microwave conforms basically to the same standards as broadcast television signals. Because of the extremely high frequencies and very low power involved, the equipment is relatively small and inexpensive. Each system is eligible to operate four channels.

A single-channel transmitter, operating much like a typical broadcast transmitter, generates the microwave carriers, modulates them with video and audio information, and transmits the signal to multiple receiver sites. At the receiver site, the signal is received by a directional microwave antenna; a downconverter changes it to a standard broadcast VHF TV channel, and it is fed to one or more standard TV sets. Each receiving site is authorized to operate a very low-power voice/data response transmitter to communicate back to the central transmitter site.

The FCC has recently authorized ITFS systems to lease their idle capacity on a profit-making basis to commercial activities. Thus, an institution operating an ITFS system for instruction on weekdays can lease its facilities during the nights and weekends to MDS operators or other business ventures.

MDS (MULTIPOINT DISTRIBUTION SERVICE)
MMDS (MULTICHANNEL MULTIPOINT DISTRIBUTION
SERVICE)

Purpose.   The Multipoint Distribution Service (MDS) was authorized as a common carrier service to provide for the commercial distribution of private television, high-speed computer data, facsimile, control information, or other communications. As common carriers, licensees neither provide nor control the programming of the system. As commercial operators, they merely lease the services of the system to others, who in turn provide and market the programming services. The MDS operates at microwave frequencies, which makes the system generally private from the general public, who must subscribe to the service to receive it. If greater security is desired for the programming, the operator may, and usually does, employ address coding/decoding or scrambling/descrambling technology. Presently, the major use of MDS is to distribute premium television programming to hotels, motels, apartment complexes, homes, etc. In a word: pay TV. There are many authorities who envision multiple-channel MDS (MMDS) as "wireless cable television."

Historical Perspective.   MDS was originally point-to-point communications within the Point-to-Point Microwave Radio Service. Operating in the 2 gHz microwave band (2150–2160 mHz), its channels were limited to 3.5 mHz bandwidths, too narrow to carry television signals (which require 6 mHz bandwidths). It was used primarily for voice and data business communications. In 1970, the FCC lifted this narrow bandwidth restriction, and immediately received numerous requests for permission to operate point-to-multipoint service to deliver television programming. By 1972, so many operators were doing this that the FCC created the Multipoint Distribution Service (MDS). It adopted the rules for MDS in 1974 as a separate service. These rules provided for two channels, each 6 mHz wide to carry TV signals, in each of the 50 largest metropolitan markets. These channels were 2150–2156 mHz (channel 1) and 2156–2162 mHz (channel 2). From 1972 to 1980, there were 1771 MDS applications filed with the FCC. By 1982, licenses had been granted for 240 stations, construction permits granted for 130 more, and there were 340 more applications pending. There were no remaining channels left for growth in the major metropolitan markets, and the demand for not only single-channel but multiple-channel systems was great.

New Developments. Under the pressures of the demand, and recognizing the further growth potential of MDS, the FCC in 1983 provided for the expansion of the service. The Commission had determined that the Instructional Fixed Service (ITFS), which had been allocated the chunk of frequencies from 2500 to 2690 mHz, was not adequately using its allocation, and displayed no inclination to do so. Therefore, the FCC transferred eight channels from ITFS to MDS. It eliminated the prior restriction of one channel per operator per market, and authorized multiple-channel Multipoint Distribution Service (MMDS). This provided for eight channels per service area, and the Commission restricted each operator (licensee) to a maximum of four channels per market. This ensures the possibility of two competing MMDS operators in any area. The same rules required that MDS protect ITFS stations already operating on those channels (grandfathered the existing ITFS stations), and permitted ITFS stations to lease their unused capacity to MDS operators. These same rules proposed a lottery system for the award of MDS licenses.

Present Status. The common carrier MDS (or MMDS) is now capable of providing up to eight channels of commercial electronic delivery service to any given area. The FCC has created an environment for growth and encourages experimentation for further development. Presently, delivery of private premium television programming (STV, PTV) is the biggest use,and many envision MDS as wireless cable. In competing with cable TV, however, MDS has several disdvantages. MDS is limited to line-of-sight transmission at its microwave frequencies, which makes it subject to the propagation idiosyncracies of microwave. Cable can provide more channels to the subscriber, and very stable and high-quality signals. Presently, MDS is highly successful for delivering pay and subscription television in areas where cable does not exist. MDS can go into an area quickly and set up operations, enjoying monopoly status in most cases. However, when cable comes to town, MDS usually suffers severe subscriber loss. Business data and services, however, appear to provide MDS with a fruitful market that may ensure its future.

Overview of the Technology. The MDS, or MMDS, service is a common carrier service designed to privately distribute television, data, or other services. The MDS system is very similar in operation and technology to the ITFS service previously described. It uses frequencies in the 2 gHz microwave band, modulated with video/audio/data information, and radiated in an omnidirectional (all directions) pattern to local subscribers. It is a one-way system. Each licensee is authorized to operate up to four channels of service in a given area.

Overview of Operation. The single station of an MDS system employs a microwave transmitter and a nondirectional antenna to transmit its signal equally in all directions. Subscribers to the service must be equipped with a highly directional microwave receiving antenna, a downconverter to convert the microwave signal to a standard unused VHF TV channel, and standard TV sets for television reception or the appropriate terminal for data use. After the signal is downconverted to a standard signal, it might be routed throughout the building to various devices via coaxial cable. Since the technology and frequencies are nearly identical to the previously discussed ITFS, the basic processes will only briefly be described here. Program security technology is the primary difference from ITFS; however, it is generally the same as discussed previously for subscription television (STV).

The Transmitter. The transmitter of the MDS system is nearly identical to the ITFS transmitter previously described. Both employ the basic technology of the broadcast television transmitter, but because of the microwave frequencies and very low power involved, MDS transmitters are much smaller and cheaper. The visual and aural sections of the transmitter generate their microwave carriers, and modulate them with the appropriate video/audio/data intelligence. The processes within the transmitter must comply generally with those standards established for broadcast television signals. Therefore, the visual transmitter employs AM modulation, and the aural transmitter employs FM modulation, creating a vestigial sideband channel 6 mHz wide, but with the carrier operating at a microwave frequency. This signal is applied to a common microwave antenna.

The Antenna. Since the MDS operates in the same frequency band (2 gHz) as the ITFS, the only difference in antennas is that the FCC requires MDS to employ a nondirectional antenna to provide service to multiple receiver sites (subscribers) in any direction. The radiating element will be about ½–¼ inch long. The FCC permits either horizontal or vertical polarization. The antenna will normally be elevated upon a tower or mast to achieve maximum line-of-sight benefits.

Coverage Factors. The coverage area of an MDS station, like ITFS, is dependent upon antenna height, power, obstacles in the signal path, and of course its inherent propagation characteristics. Both transmitter and receiver antennas are elevated to maximize the benefits of line-of-sight propagation, and to minimize the disadvantages, including obstacles which absorb or deflect the signal. The FCC limits the power of MDS and MMDS stations normally to 10 watts, but permits only the minimum power necessary to provide adequate coverage to the subscribers. Although waivers are granted, no station is permitted power in excess of 100 watts. These factors permit MDS signal coverage over a radius of approximately 25 miles, just enough to serve a local population area.

Frequency Allocation. The frequency allocation for MDS was discussed in the section on ITFS. In 1983, the FCC reallocated a segment of the

ITFS band to MDS. The MDS allocation consists of the frequencies of 2596–2644 mHz of the 2 gHz band. This segment is divided into eight channels, each 6 mHz wide to permit the carriage of television signals. Each individual licensee can operate four channels in a given market. This provides for every area being served to be served by as many as eight channels and by two competing MDS systems.

Overview of Reception. As with ITFS, the MDS signal is a standard television signal carried on a microwave carrier. The receiving site must receive as much of the signal as possible, convert it to a standard but unused TV broadcast channel, and send it to standard TV sets, or data terminals.

The Receiving Antenna. The signal is intercepted by a directional microwave receiving dish (or screen reflector) aimed toward the transmitting antenna. The maximized signal is then fed to the downconverter (see Fig. 4-6).

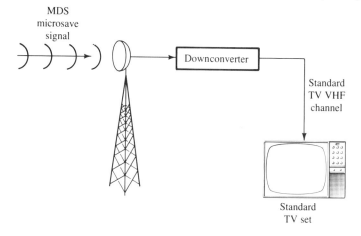

Figure 4-6 MDS receiver system.

The Downconverter. The downconverter is located near the antenna on the mast. It internally generates a predetermined frequency to mix with the incoming signal. The resulting difference frequency, complete with the modulation, is a standard VHF TV channel. Downconverters are designed that can convert four microwave channels simultaneously to four different VHF TV channels for MMDS systems.

The Receiver. The standard TV signal is sent to a standard TV set (or data terminal) for processing and display of the information. Usually, the TV signal is amplified and distributed throughout the building (if an office building) on coaxial cable to various TV/data outlets and/or recorders.

Scrambling.   When the MDS programmer desires more program security from pirating than the simple use of microwave equipment provides, scrambling technology can be incorporated. This technology is used extensively in PTV and STV applications, and is described in those sections. Briefly, during the modulation process within the transmitter, the video or sync signal (and sometimes the audio) is broken up or scrambled, and transmitted in that condition. The receiver system then requires a descrambler unit (decoder) that unscrambles the scrambled TV signal after it has been downconverted in order for the TV set (or data terminal) to be able to receive and display the signal properly. (Refer to the sections on STV and PTV for detailed discussions of scrambling/encoding techniques. See Fig. 4-7).

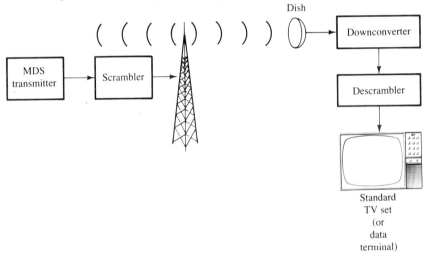

Figure 4-7   MDS scrambling system.

Addressability Security.   When the program supplier for the MDS service desires the signal to have more security than simple scrambling provides, addressability technology is employed. This technology is used extensively in cable PTV, and is also discussed in that section. When addressability is incorporated, the MDS transmitter includes in the transmitted signal a series of coded, or digital, pulses. The receiver system then must have a decoder unit that responds to the address code by permitting the downconverter signal to pass through to the TV receiver (or data terminal). Without the proper decoder, the subscriber's receiver system will not pass the signal. The coded addresses and decoder units can be changed periodically by the MDS operator to continually thwart piraters who finally break the code (see Fig. 4-8).

Combined Security.   When super security is desired, both scrambling and addressability can be employed together. The transmitter will both scramble

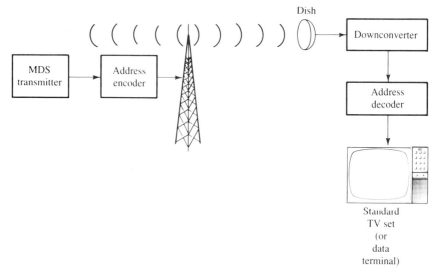

Figure 4-8 MDS addressable system.

the signal and encode it with an address code. The receiver system must then have both a decoder and descrambler unit in order to receive the signal. The received microwave signal must first be downconverted to a VHF TV channel, passed on by the address decoder, and then descrambled before being properly processed by the standard TV set (see Fig. 4-9).

Summary. The Multipoint Distribution Service (MDS) is a microwave single-point to multiple-point distribution system used for the purpose of commercially distributing TV, data, facsimile, and other services to subscribers within a localized area. An MDS operator (licensee) leases the services of the facility to a commercial entity that programs the channel and markets its services to the subscribers. Operating as a common carrier, the MDS operator provides the distribution services, but has no involvement with the programming of the system. Each market area has eight MDS channels available, with each MDS operator limited to operating four channels (MMDS) in the same area. The primary utilization of MDS systems presently is to market premium television programming to hotels, apartment complexes, hotels, homes, and the like.

An MDS transmitter transmits a standard television (or data) signal on a microwave carrier frequency. The signal is transmitted omnidirectionally over an area of about 20–25 miles radius to subscribers equipped with microwave receiving equipment. At the receiver sites, the microwave signal is intercepted by a directional antenna, downconverted to a standard VHF TV channel, and received by a standard TV set (or data terminal). Usually, for security from program pirates, the signal is transmitted in addressable or scrambled form,

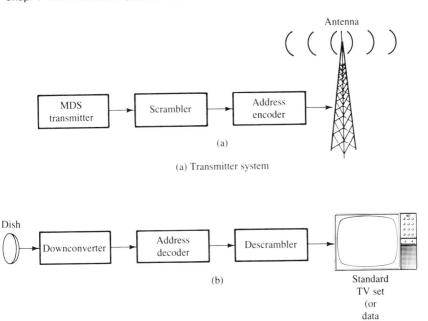

(a) Transmitter system

(b) Receiver system

Figure 4-9 Combined security. (a) Transmitter system; (b) receiver system.

requiring the proper decoder or descrambler at the receiver site. The number of receiving subscribers per channel is unlimited. Some visionaries foresee MMDS as "wireless cable television."

OFS (OPERATIONAL FIXED SERVICE)

Historical Perspective. Prior to 1963, private microwave communications came under the Fixed Service, and communications were limited to multichannel voice and data transmissions. In 1963, when creating the ITFS Service, the FCC recognized a need for businesses and municipalities to transmit video as well as voice and data in their communications activities. Therefore, in addition to existing frequencies assigned, the Commission allocated three channels in the ITFS band (2500–2690 mHz) for business video communciations, but on a secondary basis. In 1975, the Commission created what is now known as the Private Operational Fixed Microwave Service (OFS) when it removed this secondary status in the ITFS band, and in 1981 authorized on all assigned channels the distribution of products and services (including video) by licenses to their customers. This constituted a business use of video distribution, but the Commission forbade a common carrier operation of distributing entertainment programming in this service.

Subsequent Development. Subsequently, the FCC received 1400 applications from 60 different entities seeking to provide video entertainment services. In 1983, under the pressure of demand, the Commission authorized certain of the higher frequencies (in the 21 gHz area) to be used by OFS licensees to distribute their own products and services to any location of their customers, including hotels, apartments, and homes. Additionally, it laid the basis for additional lower frequencies (2.5 gHz band) to be used for this private entertainment video distribution, starting in late 1985. This relaxation of restrictions indicates that the FCC is lifting the prohibitions against the uses of OFS to transmit video programming to broadcast stations, MDS, SMATV, and cable systems in some of the higher-frequency bands. Perhaps the demand will eventually result in multiple-channel authorization similar to the development of MMDS. The OFS is, however, still a private microwave system, and common carrier activities have been specifically prohibited. OFS licensees, therefore, must still have an ownership or contractual interest in the products or services distributed.

Operational Overview. Any person, entity, or agency is eligible to apply for an OFS license to operate a private radio communication system. The purpose of such a system is generally limited to the licensee distributing its own products and services to its own customers. Therefore, the licensee cannot lease OFS service to others as a common carrier, but is required to possess an ownership or contractual interest in the programming distributed. Originally intended for the distribution of voice and data within the facilities of a corporation, the FCC has recently expanded uses to include video programming sent to customers of the licensee. The FCC has categorized usage into two general categories: short-haul systems of 250 miles or less, and long-haul systems of over 250 miles. Thus, a licensee can establish either a local directional point-to-point or nondirectional system, or a long-haul relay system between major cities. Such a system can employ a series of unmanned microwave relay transmitters (or repeaters) cross country. These systems are permitted to be interconnected with common carrier systems for the purposes of more efficient and effective transmission.

Technological Parameters. The OFS system is a low-power micro-wave distribution system. It is authorized to use numerous frequency assignments from 928 mHz to 40 gHz. It shares these bands with several other services, and therefore precautions against interference are highly important considerations in the regulation of the service. Various groups of frequencies are assigned according to bandwidth utilization. These bandwidth assignments range from channel widths of 25 kHz to 100 mHz, providing for various services encompassing audio, video, data, control, and other types of transmissions. Channels are available with paired return or response channels. The FCC rules provide tables of available frequency assignments, bandwidths, return channels, and uses. Any type of modulation is permitted, and experimentation within established parameters is encouraged. The Commission authorizes only the minimum power necessary for each station, depending upon the frequency, modulation, and application involved. Maximum limits for various combinations have been established between 5 and 20 watts. (Some older stations established prior to 1976 have been grandfathered to 30 watts.) Highly directional antennas are required of transmitters and receivers in general; however, omnidirectional facilities are permitted when justification exists. Every licensee will use all technical and operational means appropriate and available to prevent interference with other systems and services.

Summary.   The OFS is evolving from a private microwave voice and data communications system to a service resembling a private MDS. However, where MDS is a common carrier commercial operation, OFS is limited to the distribution function of audio, video, data, and control products and services between the owner-licensee and its organizational units or customers, locally or over long distances. Generally speaking, OFS might be described as private MDS systems operated by the owners of the programming distributed to their outlets or customers.

CARS (CABLE TELEVISION RELAY SERVICE)

Overview.   The Cable Television Relay Service (CARS) is not a distribution service to the general public nor to subscribers. It is a distribution service to program distributors (cable TV systems) who in turn distribute programming to the general public, or subscribers. For this reason, CARS will not be discussed in any detail; indeed, perhaps it does not belong in this book at all. However, since CARS is a distribution system of secondary relationship to programming for the general public, many of the readers may have a need for a cursory acquaintanceship with it. Thus, CARS is herewith discussed; but only in cursory manner. Reference to the section on Cable Television might be productive for a better understanding of CARS.

Purpose.   The Cable Television Relay System (CARS) was established, and serves the purpose, for the transmission of programming to cable television systems for the subsequent distribution of this programming to the general public via the cable system. [Additionally, CARS may be used to transmit programming to TV translator and low-power (LPTV) stations.] Generally, the CARS stations are authorized to pick up and relay to cable systems the signals of TV broadcast stations, AM and FM broadcast stations, ITFS stations, and cablecasting intended for use by one or more cable television systems. Although in some instances additional data, telemetry, and control signals may be transmitted in support of the operation, a CARS station will be authorized only where the principal use is the transmission of television program material or cablecasting.

Ownership.   A license for a CARS station will be issued only to the owner of a cable television system, or to a cooperative enterprise wholly owned by cable television owners or operators. CARS systems can supply program material to cable systems and translator stations only where the CARS licensee of the station or system is also the owner of the cable system supplied, or where the cable system is owned by a member of the CARS licensee organization, or where the CARS station provides the programming to the cable system on either a free or nonprofit cost-sharing basis. In short, CARS systems are not operated by independent commercial entrepreneurs, but by cable system owners and participants.

CARS Stations.   The term *CARS* actually includes three different types or uses of stations. A CARS Studio-to-Headend Link (SHL) station is a fixed microwave station located at a cable system's remote studio that transmits the studio-originated programming to the cable system headend (cable's version of the transmitter site) for distribution on the cable system. (See the section on cable television for a detailed discussion of local origination.) A CARS pickup station is a microwave mobile unit that travels to the scene of an event and transmits television signals from the scene to the cable system studio or headend. A CARS Local Distribution Service (LDS) station is a fixed microwave station within a CARS system that transmits a television signal from a local point to one or more cable systems. Since LDS stations can engage in repeater operations, many LDS stations can be used serially to relay a signal to distant cable systems.

Operational Overview.   A single cable television system might employ the three different types of CARS stations to receive programming in addition to its off-the-air and satellite sources. The system could consist of an SHL to feed its locally originated programming from its downtown studio to the cable headend outside of town. It might operate a mobile van containing a pickup station for on-the-scene local news and sports events coverage for the local origination channel, and microwave these programs to the studio for recording or feeding over the SHL to the headend. Additionally, the cable system might send to, or receive from, a distant cable system programming over a series or network of LDS stations. Most CARS stations in an LDS network are unmanned, remote-controlled stations, often in very isolated areas. CARS systems may interconnect

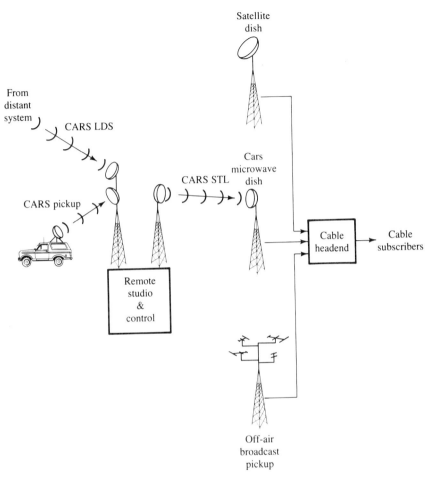

Figure 4-10   CARS system.

with other CARS systems, common carriers, and television auxiliary stations, and may retransmit their signals.

Technological Parameters.   CARS systems operate in the microwave region of 12.70–13.20 gHz, which they share with the Fixed Satellite Service (earth-to-space) and Television Auxiliary Broadcast Stations. Because of the high microwave frequencies involved (with their critical propagation considerations) and the local, or short-range, point-to-point nature of their use, CARS transmitters and receivers use extremely directional antennas. The transmitter antennas beam signals to the intended receiver, the beam width being limited to generally about 2 degrees wide. Antennas are elevated and marked, as discussed in previous technologies. The FCC limits operating power to the minimum required for the specific application, and in no event will it exceed 5 watts on any channel. Operators may employ any type of appropriate modulation (AM, FM, phase, digital, multiplex, etc.), and any polarization of the signal. The frequency allocation consists of 237 channels, which are divided into three categories, according to the type of station, its modulation, and its antenna polarization. Generally, bandwidth is limited to 12.5 mHz per channel (the equivalent of two TV channels, plus); however, waivers are permitted for specific justification.

Interference.   Protection against interference in the CARS service is paramount. Microwaves of these frequencies are rather unpredictable and unstable. The frequency band is shared with the Satellite and TV Broadcast Auxiliary Services. There are a multitude of co-channel and adjacent channel operations within the same geographic areas. It is for these reasons that the FCC requires such low-power, highly directional antennas, and other interference precautions.

Summary.   CARS is a microwave service designed for the owners and operators of cable television systems to transmit and relay television and radio programs from their point of pickup to the cable system for distribution to the subscribing public. These stations can be used as studio-to-headend links, remote pickups from the scenes of live events, or as relays to more distant cable systems. The CARS systems may interconnect as networks and with other common carrier systems whose signals they may retransmit (see Fig. 4-10).

the cable media

5

MATV (MASTER ANTENNA TELEVISION)

The Concept.   Master Antenna Television Systems (MATV) are mini-ature cable television systems within an apartment complex, hotel, mobile trailer court, and other similar facilities. The concept eliminates the necessity for apartment complexes and other multioccupant buildings to sprout rooftop TV receiving antennas for each apartment, and provides better reception for each unit than could be obtained by an individual antenna for each. Since the system is completely contained within private property and is not within the FCC's definition of cable systems, MATVs are not regulated by state or federal government.

The Operation.   The MATV system consists of a single antenna system picking up TV signals off the air and feeding them to a cable system that distributes the signals to multiple TV outlets within the complex. The antenna system is normally located on top of the building and/or on a mast or tower that elevates it above obstructions to achieve better line-of-sight reception. The better antenna installations will consist of a receiving antenna for each local channel received, and oriented toward the station. The signals from each antenna are combined together, amplified, and fed into the coaxial cable distribution system. The signals are then available at any outlet of the system for reception by standard TV sets. The system also is usually capable of reception of FM radio broadcast stations (see Fig. 5-1). Refer to the section on cable television for details on cable technology.

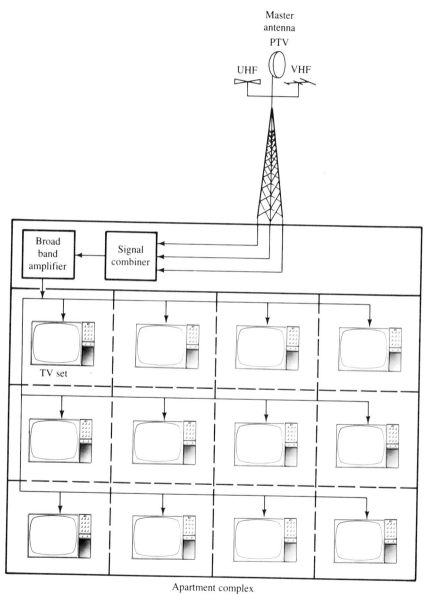

Apartment complex

Figure 5-1   MATV system.

SMATV (SATELLITE MASTER ANTENNA TELEVISION)

The Concept.   Satellite Master Antenna Television (SMATV) systems are a logical extension of MATV systems. They employ a common receiving antenna to intercept television signals to be fed into a cable distribution system serving the units of apartment complexes, motels, office building, mobile home courts, and the like. In this case, however, the antenna is a microwave dish antenna aimed skyward at a particular satellite station. This satellite "earth station" or "Television Receive Only" (TVRO) antenna system intercepts the microwave signal from the satellite, amplifies it, and downconverts it to a standard TV VHF broadcast channel. This converted signal is then combined with the MATV signals of the local stations for distribution throughout the system. It is tuned in on an ordinary TV set, just as the other signals are.

The Operation.   The hotel or apartment complex being served by SMATV might own and operate the system, and charge tenants an increased rate in rent for the service. Normally, however, an SMATV operator contracts with the complex owner to establish, maintain, operate, and market the SMATV channel to resident subscribers individually. In hotels, a pay-per-view (PPV) system is often established where a call to the hotel operator will connect the SMATV channel to a specific room during only a specific program—to be billed to the room. (Refer to the section on cable television for other methods of cable premium program service.)

Uses.   An SMATV system can be established to receive any domestic TV satellite. Most facilities use it to pick up a cable satellite to receive premium television programming intended for cable TV systems (HBO, ESPN, etc.). Many hotels are using it to provide teleconferencing sites for businesses. SMATV, especially with the added incorporation of return-channel capability (transmitting responses via the satellite) offers an exciting new area of exploitation, rapidly becoming an industry within itself—teleconferencing (see Fig. 5-2). Refer to the section on cable television for cable distribution technology, and to the section on satellites for satellite reception technology.

CATV [CABLE (COMMUNITY ANTENNA) TELEVISION]

The Need.   Cable Television, originally and often still called Community Antenna Television (CATV), developed in 1949 as a direct result of the limitations of broadcast television in reaching beyond the metropolitan areas in which the TV stations were located. Since television broadcasting was still in its infancy, TV stations tended to be located in the large cities, where the market

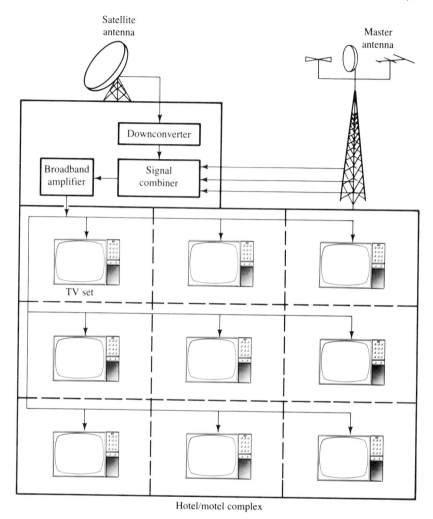

Figure 5-2   SMATV and MATV system.

could readily support them. Television was at that time assigned to the VHF band (UHF assignments were added later), which is line-of-sight transmission. The TV signals would not normally be picked up by receivers beyond the horizon, about 35 miles away, or in areas isolated from the cities by mountains. People beyond the mountains and in the valleys did not appreciate being left out and denied this marvelous new medium, and the stage was set for entrepreneurs who could extend those broadcast signals to reach these small cities, towns, and rural areas.

The First Systems.   This entrepreneurial achievement was accomplished in 1949. Authorities are divided as to whether the first system was operational in Lansford or Mahoney City in Pennsylvania, or in Astoria, Oregon. In each of the nearly simultaneous cases, events and developments were very similar. The closest television station signal was blocked by intervening mountains. Local businessmen and technicians pooled their resources, built a tall master receiving antenna atop a mountain closest to the city station where the signal was receivable, and received the faint, distant television signals. These were amplified and transported over a crude cable strung on poles down the mountainside and into town. The signal was further amplified and run throughout the town on existing utility poles. The entrepreneur charged residents an installation fee and a monthly service charge to have their TV sets connected to the cable. (In fact, the entrepreneur was often the local merchant for TV sets, and would also sell the resident a set.) Since the cable often provided comparatively good reception (compared to the alternative) of several distant stations, cable subscriptions and TV set sales were brisk. The significant fact is that cable television was developing in many places simultaneously by independent entrepreneurs (usually TV technicians) to satisfy a public demand for television where the television broadcast industry could not (see Fig. 5-3).

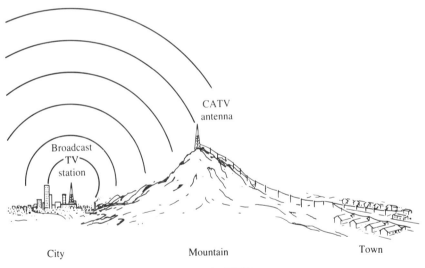

Figure 5-3   Early CATV system.

Technological Developments.   By today's standards, these early cable systems were simple and primitive. They generally could deliver only perhaps three or four channels of TV, which were usually very snowy by today's standards. The technology of cable and amplifiers, which are the heart of the system, was in the pioneering stage, and their performance was very limited. In the 1950s, technology produced coaxial (concentric) cable and amplifiers that would carry more channels and cleaner signals. During the 1960s, transistorized amplifiers and broadband coaxial cable were developed that could carry 12 TV channels with less loss. The 1970s brought technology improvements to increase cable capacity to over 30 channels, and this was expanded further to over 50 channels per cable in the early 1980s. Present-day systems can provide a delivery capacity of over a hundred channels by laying two (or more) cables side by side throughout the town to simultaneously serve each subscriber.

Economic Perspective.   During its first decade (the 1950s), cable was providing a service not only to subscribers who otherwise would receive no TV, but also to the television stations and industry. Cable increased the station's viewing audience beyond the station's own capability. The more viewers a station has, the greater its marketing base and prestige, and the more income it receives for advertising. Broadcasters loved cable. In the 1960s, however, cable systems started invading the cities, bringing improved TV signals of the local stations to the city viewers, free of ghosts and snow caused by concrete and iron skyscrapers interfering with the over-the-air signals. This, too, was all right until cable systems began to become a threat to the local stations by importing the TV signals of other distant stations into the local market to compete with the local stations in their own markets for their audiences.

Other issues began to develop besides the importation of distant signals that resulted in fractionalizing the local station's audience. Many systems did not carry one of the local stations on the cable, putting that station at an economic disadvantage with the other local stations carried. Although local stations would not televise a local sporting event in order to encourage gate attendance, sports promoters would be very upset when local viewers could watch the game on an imported distant channel, subverting local attendance. Other issues were rapidly developing. Thus ended the love affair between broadcast TV and cable, who have since been bitter rivals.

Regulatory Perspective.   During the era that broadcast television and cable television were members of a mutual admiration society (the 1950s into the 1960s), the FCC preferred to ignore cable. After all, one of the Commission's major mandates was to regulate, protect, and promote broadcasting. And if broadcasting was happy with cable, there was no need to regulate it. There was another factor to consider, of course: Cable was not a traditional service, certainly not broadcasting. Since the Commission was neither obligated nor prepared to cope with cable, it preferred to ignore it, hoping it would go away. In the mid-1960s, when cable and broadcast became enemies, however, both cable and broadcast wanted the FCC to regulate cable. Broadcasters wanted the FCC to protect them from cable. Cable systems wanted ground rules laid down so that they would have some basis upon which they could develop, compete, and grow. Both sides wanted cable regulation for different reasons. Under pressure from broadcasting, cable, Congress, and the courts, the FCC finally in 1972 issued a comprehensive regulatory structure for cable television. A few short years after the regulations were effective in bringing some sense of direction to the cable industry, and in the subsequent political and economic trends toward government deregulation, both broadcast and cable regulations have been (and are being) diluted significantly. In fact, many of these long-established regulations are falling faster than many communications scholars and lawyers can comprehend.

The Present.   Cable television has come a long way since the days of carrying three of four snowy broadcast signals down the mountainside. It has developed into not only a whole new industry, but a whole new technology. No longer just a mere extension of TV stations into the boondocks, cable now brings to city and rural areas alike new services that were undreamed of several years ago. A single system may bring its subscribers perhaps over a hundred channels of television capacity. Besides local and distant broadcast stations, the cable system now provides the subscriber with satellite networks, microwave networks, automated channels, two-way interactive channels, local origination channels, and all of the programming associated with each. The future of cable promises to provide the subscriber with more services in the areas of instrumentation, control, data exchange and transfer, and a myriad of applications not yet thought of. As systems continue to network (interconnect) and as the technology develops at ever-increasing rates, cable television's future is both fertile and challenging. There is one curious thing: It seems that the technologists are now capable of providing more channels than there are means to fill them, or demands for them.

Overview of the Technology.   A community cable television system is an electronic distribution system basically like the original systems that used a master antenna to receive an electronic signal and distribute it to subscribers over a cable strung throughout the city on existing utility poles. In addition to vast improvements upon this basic capability, however, cable now also receives signals from the microwave networks and satellite stations as well as originating its own programming. Now capable of providing more than 54 channels of capacity on a single cable, the systems often string two cables side by side to provide subscribers with over a hundred channels. This abundance of channels motivates cable operators and entrepreneurs to constantly promote and develop new services to fill the channels. This in turn promotes more diverse applications of the technology. All cable systems, however, are essentially the same in their basic configurations and operations.

The System Model.   All cable systems consist essentially of three subsystems or components: the headend, the cable network (distribution system), and the subscriber terminal. Systems differ primarily in the degree of sophistication of these subsystems and the services provided therefrom. The function of the headend is primarily to receive electronic signals from other sources (TV stations, satellites, microwave networks, local studios, etc.), convert them into cable-usable signals or channels, and feed them into the cable network system. The cable system, physically still strung on existing utility (power or telephone) poles or through underground conduit, delivers the signals to individual subscribers. To do this requires very special cable, signal divider devices, and electronic amplifiers spaced periodic distances along the cable to keep the signals amplified to usable levels. Each subscriber terminal is connected to the cable. The subscriber terminal in most systems at present consists merely of a branch of the cable coming into the premises and connecting to a standard TV set through a converter unit (box). It is the subscriber terminal that will probably develop the most in the future, as the systems include services for subscriber interactive response, personal computers, fire and burglar alarm services, and a myriad of other services.

Signal Sources.   The headend of the cable system is generally regarded as the site of the necessary receiving antennas and the associated building containing all of the signal processing equipment. Normally, there is an appropriate antenna for each signal received by the system, aimed toward the source. Additionally, if the cable system has a television production studio or automated news or weather equipment which it provides as locally originated services, these audio and video signals are fed into the headend by a separate closed-circuit cable. Often, cable systems have arrangements with other production studios (universities, public schools, and the like) or service agencies to provide programming or services over the cable system, and these video and audio signals are also fed into the headend by separate closed-circuit cable. The system inputs, then, are generally RF signals from TV stations, FM radio stations, satellites, and microwave networks, as well as video and audio signals from locally originated studios or automated equipment (see Fig. 5-4).

The Antennas.   The standard service of any cable system is to receive broadcast television signals off the air and distribute them throughout the system. A standard TV receiving antenna for each received channel is mounted on one or more tall towers to receive both VHF and UHF TV signals. Microwave signals are picked up from microwave relay stations by small parabolic dish antennas located high on the same towers. Satellite signals are received by large parabolic dishes (at least one per satellite) mounted on the flat roof of the headend building or on the ground nearby, and aimed at the satellite received. One or more FM radio antennas is also usually mounted high on one of the towers to pick up all FM radio signals in the area. (AM stations are not normally picked up and carried on the system.) All TV, microwave, and FM antennas, since they receive line-of-sight signals, are mounted high on the tower located on a high elevation, and each is oriented toward its source station. Satellite signals are received by large parabolic dishes, which must be mounted on the ground or rooftop at the headend site, and oriented toward the source satellite in the southern sky.

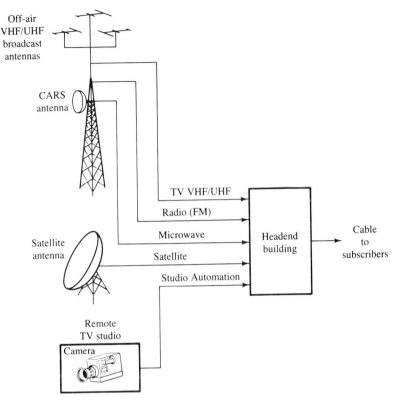

Figure 5-4 CATV system signal sources.

Sporting quite an array of various antennas of different types, many sprouting from the same tower or several towers, the antenna site is often referred to as the "antenna farm." All antennas feed their signals into the headend building for signal processing.

Signal Processing.   Coaxial cable (coax) is capable of carrying RF signals in the VHF band over great distances. It cannot, however, carry signals much above or below the VHF frequencies without great signal or energy loss. Therefore, since satellite, microwave, and UHF TV channels are frequencies too high to be carried effectively on the cable, they must be converted to VHF channels. Also, the audio and video signals coming from the studios and automated local origination sources must be converted to VHF frequencies to be carried through the cable. In other words, all signals sent through the cable must be generally in the VHF frequency range. Since only the standard off-the-air VHF-TV and FM radio signals can be carried directly, all others must be converted to VHF.

Conversion Process. The conversion of one frequency to another should remain no mystery. Very briefly, when two RF carriers are electronically mixed ("beat") together, the result is a frequency equivalent to the difference between the two originals. For example, if the carrier of one of the channels received is 600 mHz (UHF), it could be mixed in the headend with a locally produced signal of 800 mHz (also UHF) to produce the difference frequency of 200 mHz (VHF). As long as only one of the two mixing originals was modulated with sidebands, the resulting difference frequency will be modulated with that same sideband intelligence—only the carrier frequency is changed, thus changing the entire original signal to a different (VHF) channel. To convert audio and video frequencies to a VHF channel, a locally produced VHF carrier frequency (from a miniature transmitter) in the headend is modulated with the audio and video frequencies, creating a typical RF TV signal of a desired VHF channel to send through the cable. It is possible for the headend to contain and operate many miniature standard broadcast TV transmitters for this purpose because of the very tiny signal strengths involved in cable signals, and the fact that they are being used for closed-circuit cable and not broadcast operations, and are thus not technically regulated by the FCC. Through the foregoing techniques of conversion and modulation, the headend accomplishes any and all process of signals necessary to convert them all to cable-compatible VHF channels.

Channel Combining. After the necessary conversion or modulation process, the newly converted VHF signals and the naturally received VHF signals are all combined (not electronically "beat," but merely physically mixed together), amplified to the same signal strength level, and then flow through the cable network together. Thus, at any subscriber terminal, all of the TV and FM signals are available for selection by the subscriber's terminal (TV set). However, as we shall see, premium channels can be distinguished from this basic service for marketing separately to special subscribers.

Cable Capacity. Cable carriage of TV channels is generally limited to frequencies of the VHF band, plus a few more frequencies on either side. Assume, for illustration, that a cable is capable of carrying the full VHF band only. Since the VHF band extends from 30 to 300 mHz, it consists of a total capacity of 270 mHz (300 mHz − 30 mHz = 270 mHz). Since each TV channel (or signal) is 6 mHz wide, the cable has a capacity of 45 channels (270 mHz ÷ 6 mHz = 45). There are only 12 VHF TV broadcast channels (channels 2–13). Therefore, if a cable carried all 12 broadcast channels, it would have the capacity to carry an additional 33 channels for the total of its full capacity of 45. If the cable can extend its capability to just a few megahertz above and below the VHF band, this would increase channel capacity accordingly. In actuality, present "off-the-shelf" capability of cable is a frequency bandwidth of about 324 mHz, or about 54 channels (see Fig. 5-5).

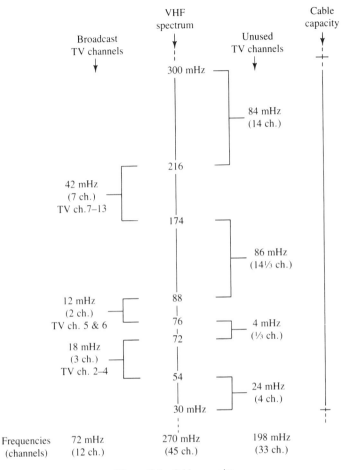

Figure 5-5 Cable capacity.

The Cable Frequency Spectrum. If we again assume for convenience cable capacity limited to the VHF spectrum of 30–300 mHz, the cable range of frequencies must be divided into segments for reference purposes. The easiest means, used by cable engineers, is to identify these segments by their broadcast channel designations as over-the-air channels are designated, and the other segments according to where they fall on the overall cable spectrum graph. Therefore, segment identification becomes: subband, channels 2–6; midband, channels 7–13, and superband. Recall that it was pointed out before that subband and superband carriage have been extended a bit beyond the VHF range, which adds a few more channels of capacity (see Fig. 5-6).

Coaxial Cable. Coaxial cable (coax), in order to carry frequencies as high as VHF (and some UHF), must be specially constructed cable. It essentially

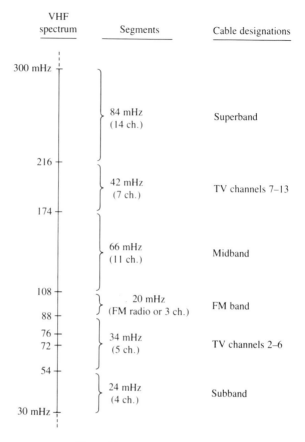

Figure 5-6   The cable spectrum.

consists of a single conductor (wire) protected by surrounding insulation running concentrically through a second conductor in the form of mesh or solid metal tubing. This arrangement is then coated with a heavy protective coating of a plastic or vinyl type of substance. Large heavy-duty cable is then often encased in an aluminum sheathing for further strength and protection. For all practical purposes, it can be said that coaxial cable comes in three size categories to serve three different phases or functions of the cable distribution system: approximately 1–1½ inches in diameter and usually aluminum clad; approximately ½–¾ inch in diameter and may or may not be aluminum clad; about ¼ inch in diameter and vinyl or plastic coated (see Fig. 5-7).

The Distribution Network.   The signals from the headend are distributed to population centers (neighborhoods or communities) on heavy-duty cable (approximately 1–1½ inches in diameter) which is usually aluminum clad, and

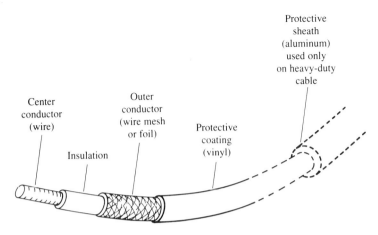

Figure 5-7 Coaxial cable.

are called the *trunk lines*. Within these neighborhoods the signals are split off from the trunk by devices called *taps* and distributed throughout the neighborhoods by *feeder lines* (about ½–¾ inch in diameter). From the feeder lines, the signals are tapped off and delivered to individual subscriber premises or terminals by plastic- or vinyl-coated *drop lines* (about ¼ inch in diameter). Most coax is strung on existing utility poles (space is rented/leased from the power or telephone company) or, where required by city ordinance, through underground conduit. Broadband amplifiers capable of amplifying the entire cable capacity of channels are spaced at intervals throughout the cable system, compensating for cable losses, to maintain a standard signal level of all channels at every subscriber terminal (see Fig. 5-8).

System Configurations.   Older cable systems and present-day small systems are designed as described above. This is referred to as a *tree branch configuration*. When the signal leaves the headend, it travels a path where it is split up between trunk lines and further divided as it travels through branching feeder lines. A newer concept is the *hub configuration*, sometimes referred to as *wheel-and-spoke*. In this model, the signal is sent from the headend simultaneously over several trunk lines, each going to a different population center, or section of town. Here, the trunk line terminates, usually at a small building, called the *hub*. The hub amplifies the signal and divides it for distribution over feeder cables throughout that section of town. Subscribers are tapped into the feeder lines by drop lines, as in the previous system. The advantage of the hub system is that the cable operator can control (turn on, turn off, or otherwise control) service to different sections of the city individually. This becomes a significant factor in sophisticated systems offering computerized services to be discussed later (see Fig. 5-9).

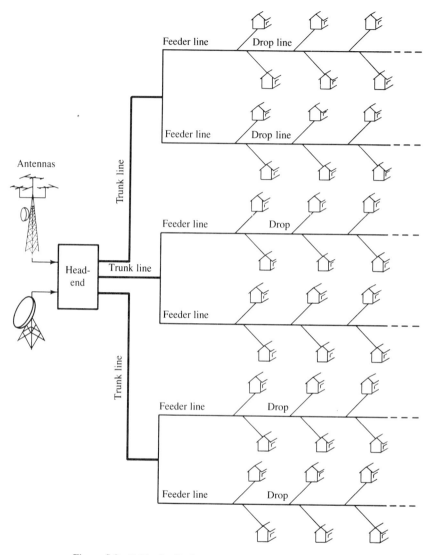

Figure 5-8   Cable distribution system (tree branch configuration).

The Subscriber Terminal.   In the typical cable system, the subscriber terminal consists of the device that the drop line coming into the subscriber's premises connects to, and which in turn delivers the signals to the subscriber's TV set. In older cable systems that carried only a few off-the-air VHF channels straight through the system with no conversion, this terminal was simple, consisting of the end of the drop cable's being connected directly to the TV set (through a very small matching transformer device). In modern systems in which

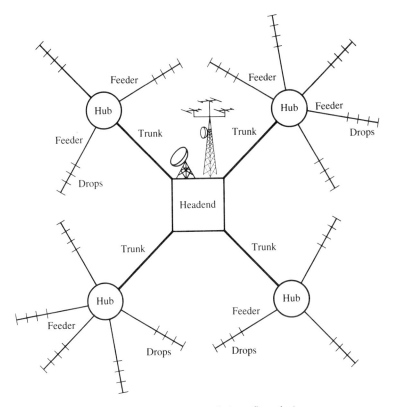

Figure 5-9 Cable system (hub configuration).

channels are converted to subband, midband, or superband channels, they must be converted back into channels that the TV set will receive, which are only the over-the-air channels the TV set tuner is preset for. Thus, there is need for a terminal in the form of a converter box that sits on the TV set. There are now TV sets designed for cable use in which a converter unit has been built in, making the TV set a "cable ready" 100-plus channel set, eliminating the need for the external converter box.

Channel Reconversion.   Whether the converter is a separate box provided (at a rental fee) by the cable company or built into the subscriber's own cable ready TV set, conversion must occur for reception of most of the cable signals. As previously described, conversion occurs by electronically mixing the desired incoming cable signal (such as a superband channel) with a predetermined frequency generated within the converter to produce a difference carrier frequency (with the original sidebands) that the TV tuner will accept (one of the standard broadcast channels the tuner is preset for). As this is done in practice, the tuner of the TV set is set to and left on a predesignated VHF channel, such as channel 3 (or another unused broadcast channel in the area). When any of the subband, midband, or superband channels are desired, the subscriber pushes the appropriate button for that channel on the converter. This activates within the converter a frequency generator that produces the exact frequency which, when mixed with the desired channel, will convert it to channel 3. Any button on the converter will generate the proper frequency to convert its associated cable channel to VHF channel 3. The channel then so converted will pass through the TV tuner when set on channel 3. If the TV set tuner is turned to any channel other than the predesignated VHF channel number (in this case, 3), the converter system will not work. The cable operator converted at the headend all channels not compatible with the cable into channels that would traverse the cable system. When the signals arrive at the TV set, the subscriber converter similarly converts those channels not compatible with the TV set tuner into channels (or a channel) that the TV tuner will accept. A complete cycle of conversion and reconversion has occurred.

FM Radio Signals.   Signals from FM radio stations are VHF frequencies (88–108 mHz) falling between broadcast VHF channels 6 and 7. Therefore, they can be received at the headend and passed through the cable system without any conversion or reconversion. At the subscriber terminal, the drop cable can be connected to a "signal splitter" device (a very small device), which sends the cable signals to both the TV converter and to the subscriber's FM radio or stereo system. The FM radio is then capable of tuning in FM stations from the cable while the TV converter converts TV channels for the TV set. Both, of course, can be used simultaneously or not. (Since AM radio signals would need to be converted to VHF to be carried on the cable, and since this would require considerable expense for very little demand, AM stations are not carried on cable systems, generally speaking.)

Another means of carrying FM radio signals is for the cable operator to select specific FM off-the-air signals he thinks that there will be a demand for, convert them to frequencies that will all fall within a specific TV channel, and then market that specific channel of FM stations separately to subscribers.

Multiple Cable Systems.   Many cable systems, in order to increase the number of channels of service to subscribers, string a second cable beside the first throughout the city. This approximately doubles the number of channels the subscriber can receive, since each cable can carry an equal but separate batch of differently programmed channels. Two drop cables come into the subscriber terminal, one labeled the A cable, and the other the B cable. Although both cables carry the same channel frequencies, the cable operator has, through headend conversion, programmed them differently. For example: channel 6 on A cable might be carrying the local channel 6 off-the-air broadcast station, while channel 6 of the B cable might be carrying HBO or some other satellite- or microwave-delivered program channel. The subscriber terminal is then equipped with an A-B switch, with which the subscriber can select two different menus of programming—the A menu or the B menu. Cable operators can, therefore, divide different kinds of programming between the cables, such as all broadcast and local origination (automated news and weather, primarily) on one cable (the basic service), and all premium programming (movie, sports, and specialty channels) on the other cable. The operator then has the option of charging the subscriber for the two cable services separately. This is one means of marketing different services separately; there are others to be discussed.

Summary. Cable systems consist of a headend, cable plant, and subscriber terminals. The headend is the site of receiving antennas which receive signals from TV stations, satellites, microwave relays, and other sources. Many of these frequencies are not compatible with the cable and are converted at the headend into cable-compatible channels. The cable plant is a network of coaxial cable that is strung throughout the city or community on existing utility poles, to which the subscribers' terminals are connected. The subscriber terminal must have a converter unit (or be a cable-ready set with a built-in converter) to convert the nonstandard channels of the cable into standard channels that the TV set will accept. Since the capacity of cable is technologically limited at present to about 54 channels, a system often lays two cables (A and B cables) side by side to serve the subscriber with more than a hundred channels of capacity.

INTERACTIVE (TWO-WAY) CABLE

General Overview. Interactive, or two-way, cable is the capability of information originating at the subscriber terminal and being sent to the headend. This provides that the subscriber can signal to or communicate with the cable operator on either an independent or a responsive basis. On a responsive basis, subscribers could respond to questions appearing on their TV screens (polling). On an independent basis, sensors in the subscriber's home could signal (by coded signal) that a fire or burglary or medical emergency was in progress; or the subscriber could query the headend for information or special programming, etc. The possibilities for service are infinite. There are basically four different methods for achieving interactive cable services: a telephone-cable hybrid system, a separate or dual-cable system, a cable loop system, or a two-way single cable system.

Telephone Hybrid System. The simplest means of interactive cable technology is not really two-way cable. It employs communication from the headend to the subscriber by the normal cable methods. The subscriber responds by regular telephone line. For example, the cable operator may lease a channel to a merchant who uses the channel to display a catalog or menu of products on the subscriber's TV screen, with item numbers and a telephone number. The subscriber can then use the telephone to call the number to order a specific product. Whether or not this can be called "interactive cable" is debatable. It certainly is not two-way cable. It is, however, effective, and does have marketable service value; it is, therefore, a viable means of interactive communication. Even a few programs on broadcast television are using the technique to poll viewers on different subjects, to which they respond by calling a designated telephone number, usually to register a vote for an unofficial and informal survey.

Dual Cable System.   It was discussed previously that cable systems sometimes consist of dual cables laid side by side, the A-B cable configuration. This is also a means of accomplishing true, two-way cable communications. Cable is stupid; it neither knows nor cares in which direction signals are flowing through it. It is the amplifiers and taps within a cable network that pass the signal in one direction only (having directional characteristics). Therefore, if the amplifiers and taps in one cable (the A cable) are arranged so that the signals are passed from the headend to the subscribers (or in the "downstream" direction), then it is only logical that if all amplifiers and taps in the other (the B cable) are installed in the reverse direction, any signal within it will travel from the subscriber's terminal to the headend (in the "upstream" direction). It merely remains to equip the subscriber's terminals with a unit which will generate electronic signals that the cable will carry: a miniature VHF transmitter. This little transmitter can then be activated by a subscriber control panel (with "yes," "no," or numerical signals) or by sensors (fire alarm, burglar alarm, gas detectors, etc.) to send these signals upstream on cable B to the headend. Thus, either responsive or independent communications can traverse the cable system from subscriber to the cable operator (see Fig. 5-10).

Cable Loop System.   A cable system employing a single cable (or dual cable) can be designed so that the trunk and feeder lines do not terminate eventually at a dead end, after having passed all subscriber premises, but terminate back at the headend. This forms a cable loop, serving the subscribers and returning to the headend. Signals originated at the headend travel downstream to all subscriber terminals and back to the headend. In this configuration, each subscriber drop line can be connected at the feeder cable by a two-way (bidirectional) tap. Signals coming downstream on the cable will flow into each subscriber's terminal. If the terminal is also equipped with a control panel and miniature transmitter as described above, the subscriber can originate and send a signal out his dropline into the feeder cable network. That signal will then travel downstream with all other signals, eventually returning to the headend, where it is received by the cable operator. (Recall that "eventually," at 186,000 miles per second, is not a very long delay.) This, too, might not be called true two-way cable, but its effect is the same, and it therefore is a viable application of the technology (see Fig. 5-11).

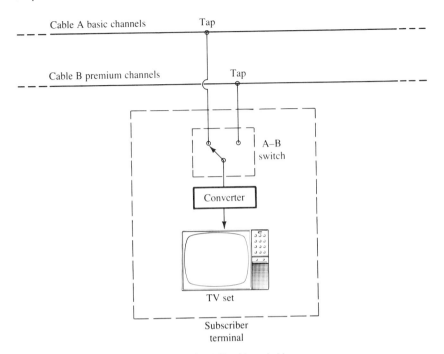

Figure 5-10   A-B cable switching.

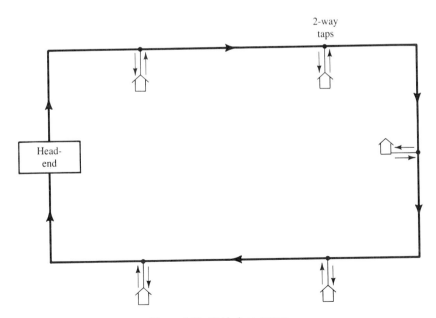

Figure 5-11   Cable loop system.

Single-Cable Two-Way System. A single-cable system (also dual-cable systems) can be designed to be a truly two-way cable; that is, different signals within the same cable can travel simultaneously in opposite directions. As was discussed previously, cable neither cares nor knows in which direction signals are traveling within it. Two different signals can travel independently and simultaneously in opposite directions through cable, depending only on in which direction its source power pushes it. It is the amplifiers and taps within the cable network that are usually unidirectional, passing all signals in one direction only while blocking them from traveling in the reverse direction. However, amplifiers can be designed to be responsive (to pass) to certain bands of frequencies and nonresponsive (to block) all others. Taps can be designed to be bidirectional, passing all frequencies or certain frequencies in both directions. Therefore, two-way amplifiers within a system can be arranged so that they will pass only certain groups of frequencies (or channels) in one direction (while blocking all others in that direction) and will pass all other frequencies in the opposite direction (while blocking the aforementioned group from that direction). If all taps are bidirectional, the system will then pass the designated groups of channels in one direction and all other channels in the other. In other words, most channels will flow downstream toward all subscribers, while a designated group of channels will flow upstream, from subscriber to headend. It merely remains for the subscribers to be equipped with miniature upstream channel transmitters and control units. In practice, the cable operator designs the system to use either the cable subband, midband, or superband frequencies for upstream (return) channels (see Fig. 5-12).

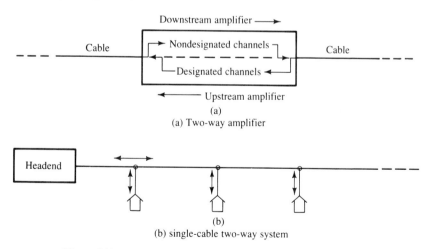

Figure 5-12 (a) Two-way amplifier; (b) single-cable two-way system.

Summary. Subscribers can interact with the cable operation through several different means. The telephone can be employed to respond to messages received on the TV screen. A separate (second) cable laid side by side with the basic cable can be designed in reverse so that subscribers receive downstream channels from the A cable and can generate channels upstream to the headend through the B cable. In a single cable system, the cable can be designed as a loop, terminating at the headend. Subscribers will receive downstream signals from the headend, and can generate signals into the cable to travel downstream back to the headend. The more sophisticated system is designed so that most channels within the cable travel downstream, but channels within a selected frequency band will travel upstream through the specially designed amplifiers and bidirectional taps. Subscribers then receive the downstream channels from the headend, and can generate signals that will travel upstream to the headend.

PAY CABLE

General Overview.   Pay cable is a service provided to the subscriber of delivering special programming for which the subscriber must pay an additional premium cost over and above the basic cable service charge. These programs might be first-run movies, special sports events, specialty programs, and similar fare. The cable operator is the middleman between the program supplier (HBO, Showtime, The Playboy Channel, ESPN, etc.) and the subscriber, supplying the physical delivery system and billing function. In some services, these special channels and programs are received continuously, the subscriber paying a monthly fee on a subscription basis. For other special program services, the subscriber receives only those particular programs (such as championship live boxing matches) which he or she desires to watch. This is a pay-per-view situation in which the subscriber pays only for those individual programs selected. The cable system can employ either or both methods of pay programming for different channels

Tiering of Services.   When a cable system provides different services for different fees, this is called *tiering* the services. Usually, the basic service provided is the first tier, consisting of the local off-the-air TV stations, some distant imported TV stations (such as Ted Turner's WTBS in Atlanta), automated news and/or weather channels (showing continually updated alphanumeric information on the screen), and perhaps channels of other local programming (public access channel, local public school channel, city government channel, etc.). For this basic service, the subscriber pays the basic monthly subscription fee. A second tier of service might consist of channels of movies, sporting events, specialty TV stations carried on satellite, and other fare which can be received constantly, like the basic service, for an additional monthly fee. A third tier might consist of service providing first-run movies or special live sporting and entertainment events of great interest. These programs would be paid for on an individual "as viewed" basis over and above any other tier subscription fees.

FM radio channels are usually proivided by the cable operator as a separate service for a separate fee.

Service Security.   The name of the game in pay television is to prevent the nonpayers from receiving the special service or premium programming. Theft of these services is an enormous problem which can cut deeply into the revenue of the program supplier, as well as the cable operator. These services are very expensive to present to the subscriber when the costs of original production, copyright fees, satellite distribution, and cable delivery are considered. Therefore, the technology of delivery of the programming is not complex: it is delivered by the same technology as previously described for cable systems in general. The technological complications come from the security measures employed to prevent the theft of services. These security technologies can be very sophisticated, complex, and expensive indeed. Many methods have been experimented with, but only a few have survived as practical. However, the incentive is constant to develop more effective means of program security.

Channel Trap Security.   Subscription pay cable is the simplest form of pay cable service. The cable headend receives a satellite or microwave signal from a program supplier and converts it to a usable cable channel. In its simplest form, the signal can be sent down the cable as a normal TV signal. Those subscribers who pay the additional cost for it receive the signal as they do all other channels of the basic service. Those subscribers who do not pay for the special channel are deprived of it by the cable operator's placing a channel trap or filter device in the subscriber's drop line (usually at the tap). This device traps out a specific channel (or small group of channels) while permitting all others to pass, thus keeping out of the subscriber terminal the premium channel he chooses not to pay extra for. If the subscriber later subscribes to the premium channel, the cable operator merely removes the channel trap from the subscriber's drop line. Since these traps are easily removed or bypassed by knowledgeable subscribers, this system of pay cable is for all practical purposes obsolete.

Scramble Security.   A more modern and effective means of securing premium program channels is through scrambling or conversion of the channel. In scrambling, the headend of the cable system receives the satellite signal from the program supplier usually in scrambled form. This is merely a means of electronically distorting the picture (and sometimes the sound) of the signal (as previously described in the section on STV). The signal is then converted, scrambling and all, by the cable operator to a usable cable channel and sent down the cable. If subscribers pay the additional fee for the channel, they are provided with descrambling units that will reconstitute the picture (and sound) as it passes through to the subscribers' converters, which convert the descrambled signal into a standard VHF signal TV sets will accept. If subscribers do not pay the extra price, no descramblers are provided, and if the subscribers tune in that particular channel, they will see merely scrambled garbage. Sometimes the program supplier scrambles the picture but leaves the sound intact, hoping that exciting sounds of scrambled programs will entice viewers to pay the price to see the programs as well as to be able to hear them.

Conversion Security.   Another means of securing premium channel programming is through conversion technique. When the headend receives the satellite signal in an unscrambled form from the supplier, it is converted to one of the subband, midband, or superband channels that requires a converter at the subscriber's terminal. If the system is a twelve-channel or less system that employs no converters because all the used cable channels are standard VHF TV channels, the subscriber must have the converter to receive the special premium channel. Subscribing to the premium channel provides for a subscriber channel converter. No pay, no converter, no premium programming. If the system already employs converters for its basic service, the cable operator can employ either of two options. He can disable the button on the standard converter that correlates to the premium channel on the converters of all nonpremium channel subscribers, while activating that button only on the converters of those who subscribe to the channel. Or he can instead employ conversion that would require a separate individual special converter for the premium channel. This second special converter would be provided only to subscribers of the premium channel.

Hybrid Security.   The cable operator has the technical capability of using either or both scrambling and conversion methods simultaneously. If the headend receives an unscrambled satellite signal, the cable operator could conceivably scramble it himself, or not, and send it down the cable, requiring additional conversion, or not. Similarly, if the headend receives a scrambled signal from a satellite, the operator could conceivably descramble it, or not, and send it down the cable, requiring additional conversion, or not. In other words, the cable operator technically has the control of using either or both or neither the scrambling and conversion security techniques. The cable operator's options, however, in actuality are limited by contractual agreements with the program supplier.

Pay-Per-View (PPV): One-Way Cable.   The simplest form of pay-per-view premium service occurs with the one-way cable system. When the subscriber sees an advertisement (on TV or in the newspaper) of a special program upcoming on the pay-per-view (PPV) channel, he or she calls the cable operator on the telephone and requests to view the program at the scheduled time. The subscriber's terminal must be equipped with a special decoder unit. When the program is sent down the cable, it is preceded by a coded digital signal (like an electronic key) that activates or turns on the subscriber's special decoder. The program is followed by a coded digital signal which deactivates or turns off the decoder. Each subscriber decoder unit has its own built-in or programmed digital address or lock. The headend precedes the special program with the coded signals of the digital addresses of each subscriber ordering and paying for the program, which unlocks or activates each of these boxes without disturbing nonpaying subscribers. If a nonpaying subscriber turns his converter to the pay channel, the screen will be blank during the duration of the special PPV program. The digital locking and unlocking of subscriber decoders is done by computer from the headend, which can rapidly handle large numbers of subscribers. Each neighborhood or hub may be handled by a separate computer if the number of system subscribers is extremely large, or if the operator chooses for some other reason to operate each population area differently.

Pay-Per-View (PPV): Two-Way Cable.   The two-way cable PPV system works essentially similarly to the one-way cable system. The subscriber request for viewing a program is done through the cable, however, instead of externally by telephone. In this system, the subscriber's terminal is equipped with an addressable decoder unit, but which also contains a miniature VHF transmitter. When the subscriber desires to view the pay channel, he or she activates a control on the decoder, which sends its digitally coded signal address to the headend by upstream channel. The headend computer recognizes the signal and sends back downstream the electronic coded address which activates (unlocks) that subscriber's decoder. At the end of the program, the computer automatically sends down the appropriate coded signals to deactivate (lock) the box. While the decoder box is unlocked, of course, it can receive the decoded channel in the same manner as the terminal receives all other channels. Of course, the upstream command from the subscriber to the computer also causes the computer to automatically bill the proper subscriber for the program.

Computerized Pay Cable Systems.   The computer and digital electronics are taking over the pay-per-view industry. Integrated circuits, micro- and superchips, and increasingly sophisticated micro- and minicomputers are making possible addressable subscriber terminals (and taps) for numerous and probably unimagined individualized subscriber services. Complementing that, these same technologies are making the upstream interactive possibilities almost limitless. The capability of each terminal to receive addressed messages and to send addressed messages upstream (or downstream) creates the potential for each subscriber to communicate directly, through various modes, with the headend, the operators of leased channels, or with any other individual subscriber. The service potential begins to stagger the imagination.

Summary. Pay cable is special programming conveyed to the subscriber, for an additional fee, via the cable technology. However, new sophisticated technology must be employed to protect the security of the pay channels from the nonsubscriber to the pay channels. Programming on these pay channels can be sent downstream as a scrambled signal. Or it may be converted to a special channel that the subscriber terminal is not equipped to process. The subscriber must then pay an additional fee to receive a descrambler or special converter box in order to enjoy the premium programming. Another form of pay cable, pay-per-view (PPV), permits the subscriber to view and pay only for specific programs on a premium channel. Digital and computer technology permit the subscriber to telephone a request, or to generate a uniquely coded signal upstream to the headend computer. When the program is sent down the cable, the computer will send a preceding and proceeding coded signal "addressed" to the proper terminal which will activate the decoder/converter at the program start, and deactivate it at program end. Digital and computer technology permit each terminal to be individually addressable and to handle innumerable subscribers, as well as permit each subscriber to individually address the headend with informative messages.

the satellite media

6

SATELLITES

Satellite Overview. The field of satellites, or man-made platforms orbiting the earth, is extensive, sophisticated, and intriguing. Satellites are used for many diverse purposes: scientific research, weather monitoring, surveillance, navigation, military functions, experimentation, communications, and many other purposes. Many orbit the earth at tremendous speeds, circling the globe several times a day in different paths, while others are in fixed orbit, appearing stationary above the earth. They are owned individually by different governments, international consortiums, private owners, and commercial enterprises. Satellites are subject to international and national law. They are the epitome of the leading edge of technology. They are a new frontier for science, law, economics, communications, and various other disciplines. In short, the world of satellites is vast and relatively uncharted. Because of the vastness, vagueness, and complexity of the field of satellites, this discussion is limited to the technology of U.S. domestic communications satellites. However, most of the discussion will be applicable as well to all satellites, and particularly to all communications satellites—domestic and international.

The Satellite Function. A communications satellite is a space station that remains relatively stationary above the earth. It serves as a platform for radio relay stations (transponders) which receive radio signals beamed to it from earth, and relays those signals back to other locations on earth. Since the altitude of the satellite permits it to "see" one-third of the earth's surface, it is possible to relay a signal from any point in this area to another single point, multiple points, or to blanket the entire area with the signal. In actual practice, the antennas on board the satellite are usually designed to concentrate its transmitted energy within a designated area, such as a continent, a country, time zone, region, or other geographic or political area. This area of the earth over which the satellite spreads or transmits its signals is called the satellite "footprint" (see Fig. 6-1).

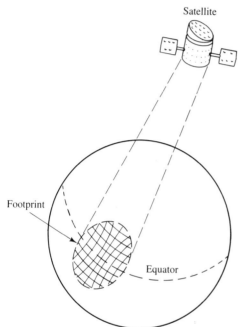

Figure 6-1 Satellite "footprint."

Advantages of Satellite Communications.   Satellite communications have proved to be an extremely advantageous means of long-distance communications. Their line-of-sight characteristics over great distances means a one-hop relay over thousands of miles, rather than many short relay hops over terrestrial microwave links, wire, or coaxial cable. Less processing and handling of the signal is required, and a cleaner signal with less noise and distortion results. Line-of-sight spacial communications requires very low power to transmit a signal from earth to satellite and satellite to earth, which results in great economic benefit over using much higher-powered terrestrial stations and multiple relays. (It takes about 75 terrestrial microwave relay stations to get a signal from New York to Los Angeles, while it takes only one satellite relay for the same distance.) Satellites can (and do) employ extremely high microwave frequencies which permit very wide channel widths to convey a lot of information on each channel. Each channel is capable of TV, high-speed data, multiple radio and telephone subchannels, and other information handling. Additionally, the nature of these microwave frequencies makes them nearly immune from atmospheric and other natural interference. In spite of the tremendous costs of the technology, satellite communications are cheaper, faster, cleaner, and more efficient and effective than traditional long-distance terrestrial communications systems.

Historical Perspective. Satellite communications began the first time that scientists bounced a radio signal off the moon (our natural satellite) back to earth. In 1960, a 100-foot-diameter metallic balloon (Echo I) was launched into space, from which radio signals were bounced back to earth. Its low orbit caused it to travel faster than the earth's rotation, and communications were limited to those periods when the balloon was within visibility. Theoretically, if an orbiting body were at a specific altitude, positioned over the equator and orbiting in the same direction as the rotation of the earth, its speed and course would be synchronous with the earth's rotation and it would appear stationary over the earth. In 1963, a satellite (Syncom) was launched which proved this theory.

In 1964, a consortium of nations formed an organization (Intelsat) to establish an international system of satellite communications. It launched the first in a series (Early Bird) in 1965. Canada launched the first commercial domestic satellite (Anik) in 1972, which carried 12 radio repeater stations (transponders) for voice, video, and data. The first U.S. domestic communications satellite (Westar I) was launched in 1974; the following year it carried the first lengthy continuous television program (a baseball game). In 1975, a 24-transponder satellite (Satcom I) was launched, on which a new pay TV service (HBO) distributed its programming to cable systems throughout the country. This rejuvenated a sagging cable TV industry, opened new horizons for satellite entrepreneurs, and Satcom I became known as the "cable bird."

The disappearance in space of a launched satellite in 1979 (Satcom III) did not dampen the satellite industry; that year the Public Broadcasting System (PBS) began distributing its programming to its affiliate stations nationwide via satellite. Subsequently, but slowly and cautiously, commercial radio and television networks began leaving the AT&T terrestrial systems for satellite distribution of their programming to their affiliates. To come full circle, the first U.S. communications satellite (Westar I) died in 1983 after nine years of service (two more than was expected).

Geographic Groupings. Satellites can be grouped into three categories according to the geographic area served. The international group of satellites provides communications around the globe and between nations. This group includes the Intelsat series, serving 135 countries, and the Marisat and Marecs systems for ship-to-ship and ship-to-shore maritime service. Regional satellites provide neighboring nations with a common system of communications among them. These include the regional systems operated by 20 European nations

(Entelsat), Arab nations (Arabsat), Eastern bloc systems, Scandinavian systems, and others. Domestic satellites are those serving a single nation, such as Canada's Anik series, India's Insat, France's Telecom, Indonesia's Palapa, and other domestic systems. The United States has several series of domestic communications satellites: Westar (Western Union), Satcom (RCA), Comstar (AT&T), SBS (Satellite Business Systems), and Galaxy (Hughes). This book will consider only U.S. domestic communications satellites, although the technological principles apply equally to all satellites.

Satellite Components.   A communications satellite is launched into space aboard a rocket vehicle, placed into an orbit of the earth that makes it appear stationary to the earth, and controlled throughout its lifetime by a ground control station that monitors and controls it continuously. The translator stations aboard can then be operated as communications relay stations as long as the platform remains aloft, its solar batteries alive, and its equipment intact. It can be readily seen that there are three distinct aspects to a satellite: the launch function or vehicle, the platform function or vehicle, and the communications function or systems. It is possible for a single entity to own and operate all of these functions, but economics, technological sophistication, and practical considerations make partnerships, joint ventures, and other contractual arrangements more realistic. One organization might launch the bird, another control it, and another operate its communications functions. In fact, whoever owns the communications transponders can operate, lease, or sell them to others.

Geosynchronous Orbit and Control.   A satellite is launched by a rocket vehicle to place it at or near the proper altitude of 22,300 miles above the earth at the equator. Compare this distance with the distance of 100–150 miles altitude that our astronauts go into space, and one gets an appreciation of the distances involved in satellite technology. After the satellite is separated from the rocket, the ground control crew propels it by means of its own small on-board rockets into exact orbiting position.

The rockets can then be turned off, and the original momentum of the satellite is maintained in near-frictionless space. At this altitude and speed, the satellite orbits around the distance of the earth once every 24 hours. Since the earth also rotates once every 24 hours, and since both are rotating in the same direction, the satellite appears to remain stationary above the earth. This is referred to as *synchronous, geosynchronous*, or *geostationary orbit* (see Fig. 6-2).

Over a period of time, the satellite may slightly lag or drift from its exact orbit position, but ground control will immediately trigger a spurt from one of its on-board minirockets and make a correction. Ground control can in this way always assure the proper position of the satellite. Further, ground control can move the satellite to another orbit position if the need should ever arise (which

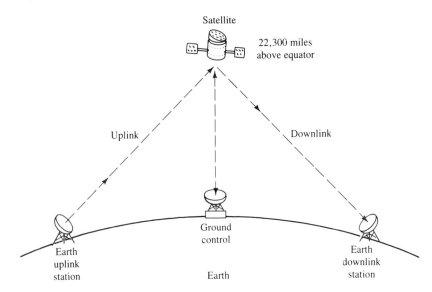

Figure 6-2   Satellite system.

has happened in the past). After the satellite's usable lifetime, or in case it dies an early death (batteries die, etc.), ground control will boost the satellite further out into space into that perpetual floating junkyard in the sky.

Satellite Design Considerations.   The design of a satellite is a matter of compromises. The designers must include the basic requirements of the platform itself: physical plant, steering rockets and fuel, solar batteries to power the communications payload, altitude control, environmental control, telemetry and control electronics for ground control, etc. Additionally, they want to include as many transponders and antennas as possible to make the payload economically profitable. However, the more that is included, the heavier and bigger the satellite must be. This means greater expense for launch, shorter satellite life due to drag and gravity, and less economic viability. Consider just one aspect: the solar batteries. More batteries provide longer life for the equipment and make more equipment possible, but add more weight to make the cost of launch higher and the controllable lifespan shorter. Optimizing compromises must be made. Presently, typical satellites can carry 24 transponders for a usable satellite lifetime of about nine years. The present lead time for the design and construction of a satellite before it can be launched is three to four years. Technological advances are, however, rapidly decreasing both of these limitations.

Transponder Capacity.   Each transponder on board the satellite consists of a small microwave receiver and transmitter powered by solar batteries. In most satellites, these microwave transmitters are very low power, less than 10 watts. Generally, each transponder has a frequency bandwidth, or channel width, wide enough to contain the equivalent of one color TV channel, 600 radio programs, 1200 telephone circuits, high-speed data circuits, or proportional combinations of these services. A typical satellite carrying 24 transponders could then relay 24 TV signals, more than 14,000 radio programs, nearly 29,000 telephone calls, innumerable data services, or combinations thereof. The capacity for intelligence relay of a satellite is rather awesome, and is increasing rapidly; yet the demand for satellite channels increases.

DOMSATS (DOMESTIC SATELLITE SYSTEM)

The System.   All satellite communications systems operate in essentially the same way. This is much like a one-hop terrestrial microwave system without the distance limitation of the horizon. A ground transmitter station accepts a radio signal (TV, voice, video, data, etc.) from a terrestrial origin, converts it to a satellite microwave carrier frequency, and beams it up to the satellite. This process is called the *uplink*. The satellite transponder (receiver section) receives the signal and converts it to a different microwave carrier frequency. The transponder (transmitter section) then transmits the microwave signal back to earth, the signal covering a particular footprint area designed into the satellite transmitting antenna. This signal can be received by any proper receiving site within the footprint area. The process of transmission from satellite to earth is termed the *downlink*. Once the signal is received by an earth station, it might use it or convert and distribute it to other users.

Uplink Earth Station.   There are two general types of uplink stations: fixed and mobile. The fixed station is generally located strategically between or near multiple population centers that have a high traffic of communications activities. Originating agencies send their signals to the uplink station. There, the signals, in whatever form, are modulated onto the appropriate satellite microwave carrier frequency and beamed up to the proper satellite. The transmitting antenna is normally a huge microwave dish, perhaps 10 to 30 feet in diameter, aimed directly at the satellite. The dish is large to increase the efficiency and effectiveness of focusing the microwave energy into a highly concentrated beam aimed at the satellite, to reduce the power required. Small mobile uplink stations are a relatively new development. These are uplink stations employing much smaller dish antennas and mounted on trailers pulled by vehicles, or on flatbed trucks. These are becoming popular for large TV broadcast stations and production organizations for electronic newsgathering or other live reporting or presentation functions from sites remote or distant from a distribution facility. These units are often called SNG (satellite newsgathering) units, as opposed to the familiar and traditional ENG (electronic newsgathering) units (see Fig. 6-3).

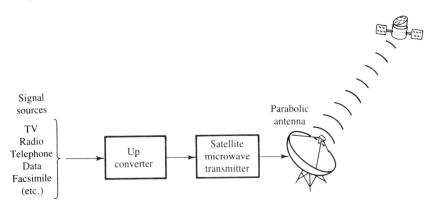

Figure 6-3 Satellite uplink (transmitter) earth station.

The Transponder.   Although a satellite may carry 24 transponders, each transponder operates on a different pair of microwave channels. A single transponder consists of a microwave receiver, a converter, and a microwave transmitter, with associated antennas, powered by solar batteries. The satellite is continuously oriented by ground control so that the solar panels are directed sunward and the antennas are directed earthward. The concentrated signal from the uplink ground station is received by the proper antenna and receiver on board the satellite, and converted to a different (lower) microwave channel. This is done to prevent the incoming and outgoing signals from interfering with each other. The low-power transmitter then transmits the signal earthward, its antenna designed to produce a particular footprint or geographic coverage area on earth (see Fig. 6-4).

Downlink Earth Station.   Any earth station, properly equipped, within the satellite's footprint can receive the satellite signal. The earth station consists of a receiving dish antenna, a special low-noise amplifier (LNA), and a microwave receiver and downconverter. The receiving dish must be aimed at the satellite and have a clear line-of-sight path (unobstructed by buildings, etc.) to the satellite. The required size of the dish is determined both by the microwave carrier frequency and the strength of the satellite signal. High frequencies and strong signals require smaller dishes. Dishes presently range in size from about 2½ to 10 feet in diameter. The signal received by the antenna is processed through the LNA to increase its strength and signal-to-noise ratio (signal level above noise level), converted to a standard TV channel or other lower frequency by the downconverter, and then demodulated into its usable intelligence or distributed to a using agency in a standard form by other terrestrial distribution systems (see Fig. 6-5).

Earth Station Antennas.   The microwave signal from a satellite must be received by a parabolic dish antenna, aimed directly at the satellite, with an

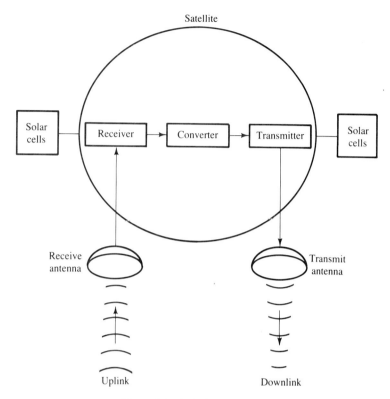

Figure 6-4 A single transponder.

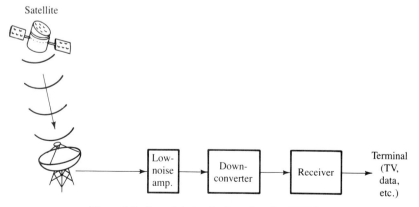

Figure 6-5 Downlink (receiver) earth station (TVRO).

unobstructed line-of-sight path. The dish gathers in and concentrates the radiated energy for the receiver. Until fairly recently, satellite dishes had such a highly directional quality that aiming at the satellite was extremely critical and difficult; a dish aimed at one satellite could not pick up the signal from an adjacent satellite. Technological improvements in the antenna design have recently, however, produced dish-type antennas that can "see" or pick up the signals from as many as four or five adjacent birds simultaneously. This alleviates some of the problem of having a separate antenna for receiving each desired satellite, or having to reorient the dish to pick up a different satellite. Although presently available, multiple satellite dishes are not yet in common use.

Television Receive-Only (TVRO) Earth Stations.   Although some earth stations possess both transmitters and receivers for uplink and downlink capability, most are receive-only stations. Receiver earth stations have been springing up all over the country to pick up television program signals from various birds. Most cable TV systems, many hotels and motels, and lots of private homes have television receive-only (TVRO) dishes aimed toward the southerly skies to intercept the programs of HBO, ESPN, and other premium pay TV services, superstations, and specialty networks. With the promise of direct broadcast satellites to soon become reality, it is conceivable that rooftop or backyard TVRO dishes will be as commonplace in the future as ordinary broadcast rooftop antennas were before cable. This becomes more practical as technology brings the size of these dishes down to less than 2½ feet in diameter.

Classification of Satellites.   All domestic communications satellites fall into one of three classifications. These classifications are based primarily on the power of the transponders of the satellite, but also correlate with the frequencies assigned and, to a lesser extent, with usage. Since power and frequency of the satellite transponders determine the size of the receiving dish antenna, these factors help determine the use to which they can be put. Satellites are classified as C-band, K-band, or DBS satellites.

C-Band Birds.   All of the low-power satellites are called *C-band satellites*. They are used generally for common-carrier (commercial communications) purposes. The name comes from the microwave band in which they operate. Microwave bands are labeled alphabetically to facilitate reference among them. These C-band birds operate with uplink frequencies in the 6 gHz region and downlink frequencies in the 4 gHz region of the spectrum, both within what is known as the *microwave C-band*. C-band transponders operate within a power range of 5 to 10 watts. This low-power consumption enables the birds to carry typically 24 transponders. New birds, however, are capable of carrying 36 transponders, with 54 possible in the near future. The low power and relatively low microwave frequencies require fairly large microwave dishes for earth station reception. These have been previously as large as 30 feet in diameter, but technological advances have reduced this requirement to first, diameters of 8 to 10 feet, and subsequently to 5 to 6 foot diameters presently.

K-Band Birds. The medium-power common-carrier satellites operate within the K-band of the microwave spectrum—hence their name of K-band satellites. These birds carry transponders that operate in the 14 gHz region for uplinks, and 12 gHz for downlinks. Note that all satellites operate on higher uplink frequencies and lower downlink frequencies. One of the reasons for this is to facilitate reconversion, or downconverting, of the signal at the receiving site. Transponder power of K-band satellites is generally in the 40–50 watt range. This higher power requirement demands more solar panels and batteries, for which transponder space is sacrificed. K-band birds therefore generally carry only about ten transponders each.

Advantages of K-band satellites over C-band birds result from both the higher frequencies and higher power, which result in less interference from ground microwave systems, stronger signals and therefore smaller earth station receiving dishes. Dishes for receiving signals from K-band satellites are approximately 2 to 3 feet in diameter. A disadvantage of K-band is, however, a greater susceptibility to "rain fade," or absorption of some signal strength by heavy rain. Performance during hurricanes has, however, indicated that this may not be a significant disadvantage.

Hybrid Birds. Although this is not a separate classification, satellites are becoming more and more hybrid by carrying a mix of C-band and K-band transponders. This permits a satellite to offer more different services and advantages than before, or to be more versatile. This trend is increasing, which generally improves the service capability of a satellite, but at the same time creates administrative and regulatory problems.

DBS Satellites. A recent development has been the authorization of high-power satellites for direct broadcasting services (DBS) to the general public. Although no high-power DBS satellites are yet in orbit (as of August, 1985), the first launch is expected in 1987 or 1988. DBS will operate in the K-band of 12 gHz (and perhaps 17 gHz). Power of the transponders will be in the range of about 150 to perhaps 300 watts. Plans anticipate that the typical DBS bird will carry three transponders, but some on the drawing boards are designed to carry six. The high power and high frequency of the DBS transponders will permit the use of small home-type earth station dish antennas (TVROs) less than three feet in diameter. DBS regulations and practices are presently extremely vague, and DBS will be discussed more explicitly in the following section.

The Satellite Parking Lot. United States domestic communications satellites must be positioned, or "parked," precisely 22,300 miles directly over the equator and in an area relative to being over the continental United States, Alaska, Hawaii, and territorial possessions. This is the only way that they will be synchronous, or geostationary, to provide a continuous and reliable national communications system. This also holds true, however, for the satellites of Canada, Mexico, the Latin and South American nations, as well as some international satellites. All must share the same parking lot. Additionally, since satellites, like terrestrial stations, must have some distance separation to avoid interference, the number of parking spaces in this parking lot are limited. International treaty was required to establish general parameters for satellite placement (or parking reservations) and use over the American continents.

Satellite Spacing. The number of satellites that can occupy spaces in this equatorial parking lot is determined by how closely to each other they can be positioned. Spacing, in turn, is dependent upon the power and frequencies employed. The United States has been assigned a total of 113 parking spaces for its domestic satellites. Of these, 35 are available for low-power C-band satellites, 70 are available for medium-power K-band satellites, and eight are allotted for high-power DBS satellites. C-band satellites were originally spaced 4 degrees apart in orbit; however, the proliferation of satellites and technological refinements have permitted reducing this spacing to 2 degrees, theoretically doubling the number of satellites that can be parked. K-band satellites, originally separated by 3 degrees, are now at 1-degree spacing. DBS satellites are anticipated to be spaced 9 degrees apart. At 22,300 miles in space, one degree equals approximately 460 miles (see Fig. 6-6).

DBS (DIRECT BROADCAST SATELLITE)

Overview. The Direct Broadcast Satellite (DBS) Service was established to provide a means whereby television signals of a broadcast nature can be originated from a single site and broadcast to all of the general public directly within the footprint area of the satellite. This would permit a television entrepreneur to uplink a TV program to a DBS satellite from which it would be blanketed on downlink over a wide footprint area. Presumably, all homes and businesses could receive the signal directly with very small and inexpensive rooftop-type dish antennas, and downconvert the signal to be received on standard TV sets. DBS operators could distribute "free" advertiser-supported or pay (scrambled) TV program services to the general public within a particular region or, by two or three satellites, to the entire nation.

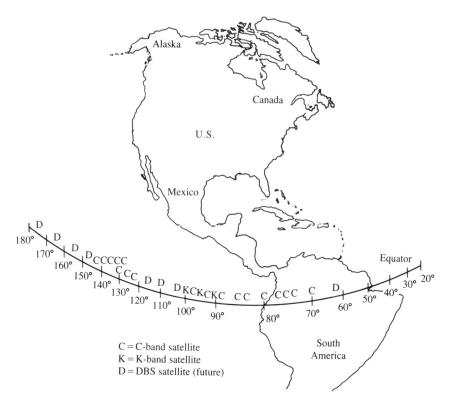

Figure 6-6 Approximate locations of U.S. DOMSATs.

Historical Perspective.   The FCC began consideration of DBS in 1980, and in mid-1981 released proposed policies and conditions to govern the authorization of interim DBS services. In October 1981, the Commission accepted applications from eight companies for DBS construction permits. This seemed premature, since the international body that would establish operating parameters for DBS services was not scheduled to meet until 1983. However,the FCC felt that an interim proposal would prepare the United States better for the international conference, but accordingly left the proposal extremely vague and flexible. The international conference in 1983 allocated to the United States eight orbital slots (satellite parking spaces) and 32 channels for DBS service. Thereupon, the FCC gave the eight applicants the green light to proceed in developing DBS proposals and capabilities.

Regulatory Perspective.   In order to facilitate the development and growth of DBS, and because of an inability to cope with new technological development, the FCC left the regulatory structure for DBS purposely vague and flexible; in fact, the FCC rules and regulations governing DBS are just a bit over two pages long. The Commission established no ownership restrictions or technical standards, but intends to process each proposal on its individual merits. The FCC did, however, levy a "due diligence" requirement that the eight applicants must have firm contracts by July 17, 1984, for construction of their DBS systems or lose their construction permits.

Hesitant Development. The economic realities of high capital requirements and high risks in DBS ventures dwindled the original eight applicants. Only four applicants apparently met the FCC's "due diligence" deadline with financial commitments; however, the Commission approved only two of them. The remaining applicants either allowed their permits to expire, or have modified their proposals and await eligibility for a second round of applications. Many of those who are applicants or potential applicants are additionally devising contingency plans for utilization of their satellites in the event that DBS does not prove to be an economically viable service. Because of the high investment required, necessarily changing standards, competition from other technologies, undetermined marketplace, and a myriad of other risks, it would seem that DBS might be a tentative service, at best.

The DBS Satellite. The DBS satellite is a high-power satellite operating in the K-band, and is used to relay broadcast programming from satellite directly to the homes of the general public. It is similar in construction and operation to other communication satellites. It operates with an uplink in the 17 gHz band (17.3–17.8 gHz) and a downlink in the 12 gHz band (12.2–12.7 gHz), with 500 mHz of spectrum for channel width of each link. Transmitter power of its transponders is authorized between 150 to 300 watts. Because of the high power of these satellites, their signals will be receivable by dish antennas approximately 2½ to 3 feet in diameter. The typical DBS bird is presently designed to carry three transponders, but some anticipate carrying six. Typical cost of a six-channel DBS satellite is estimated at approximately $80 million. Expected serviceable lifetime of a satellite is seven to ten years. Lead time of these satellites is generally about four years from drawing board to launch. The first satellite was originally expected to be launched in late 1984 or early 1985; however, the financial realities involved have delayed this expectation until 1987 or 1988.

The DBS System. The geographic area covered by the 50 states of the Union is vast. The area including its possessions and territories is even greater. Even though a satellite can "see" one-third of the earth's surface, a single DBS satellite would not be practical to cover this vast area with its footprint. There are too many time zones to be spanned, and the satellite signal would be spread too thin to be receivable by a small dish antenna. The only practical solution to cover the entire United States and possessions with a single signal is to space three or four DBS satellites approximately equidistant over the entire area, concentrate the footprint of each bird to cover only adjacent areas of one or two time zones, and broadcast the signal over the individual birds at different real times that would coincide with identical local times within each time zone region. Although a three- or four-satellite system is a tremendous investment, it could provide three to six channels of broadcasting to each and every household in the United States. This is generally the concept of present proposals for national networking by DBS (see Fig. 6-7).

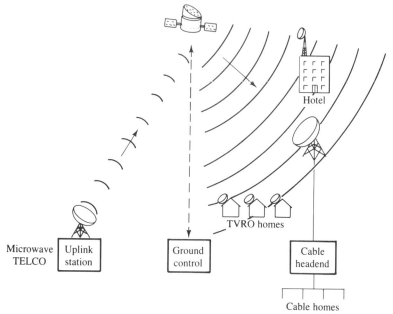

Figure 6-7   DBS system operation.

Regulatory Structure.   The FCC adopted a philosophy that would permit DBS operators to determine the nature of their services and therefore the regulatory structure under which their individual operations would be regulated. Operators who offer broadcast services themselves via the satellite will be subject to broadcast rules. Operators who lease the satellite to others for the purpose of broadcasting will be regulated under common-carrier rules. Operators who operate some of the transponders for broadcasting themselves while leasing other transponders to others will be subject to different rules for the different transponders, as applicable. In July of 1984, however, the courts determined that the FCC could not categorize a broadcast service as a common-carrier function. Much remains to be resolved in the area of DBS regulation.

Low- and Medium-Power DBS. The DBS service is authorized to use high-power satellites in order to permit the general public and homeowner to use small and affordable receiving dishes. The low-power C-band and medium-power K-band satellites were not considered practical for DBS service, since considerably larger dishes are required to receive an adequate signal. However, it is interesting to note that at least three enterprising organizations have decided to get a jump on the DBS industry by not waiting for the high-power DBS birds to be launched, and by testing the water for establishing low- and medium-power DBS service from existing C-band and K-band satellites. One U.S. start-up company leased a transponder on Canada's Anik C-II bird and established a medium-power K-band DBS service for pay (subscription) television programming serving an area of the northeast United States. This has grown to a five-channel operation serving 24 northeastern states. In 1984, two newly created pay TV DBS services were launched by leasing two separate transponders on Westar V, a low-power C-band satellite. The industry is watching these experiments closely, and the Court of Appeals has supported the use of the low- and medium-power satellites for DBS services.

Summary. Communications by satellite are generally cheaper, faster, and technically more efficient than are long-distance communications by terrestrial microwave, coaxial cable, or wire systems. A communictions satellite consists of a platform in geostationary orbit which houses several microwave relay stations (transponders). The satellite can provide a one-hop relay of an electronic signal from one site to another over the distance of one-third of the earth's surface, or can blanket a large segment of such an area with the signal. Typical satellites carry 24 transponders, each of which is capable of relaying a single TV program, 600 radio programs, 1200 telephone calls, enormous amounts of high speed data, or combinations of these. Direct broadcast satellites (DBS) are now authorized to provide direct-to-home communications, receivable by 2½ feet in diameter dish antennas. Although the regulatory, utility, and economic aspects of satellites are as yet far from being resolved, satellite communications is a new frontier, promising extended horizons for development in many technologies and disciplines.

the electronic publishing media

7

TELETEXT

Overview. Teletext is a means of providing the television broadcast station with the capability of delivering to its viewers additional or ancillary picture information, which can either be associated with or distinct from its main television program. This service can provide to the home audience the delivery of program-related information to special audiences, such as closed-captioning or foreign language subtitling simultaneously with the main channel TV program for the hearing impaired or a foreign language-speaking audience. Or, for the general audience, it can provide non-program related full-screen display of information such as catalog pages of merchandise, offerings of services, air/bus/train schedules and fares, theater/sports schedules and prices, and many other types of information. Among other purposes, this can provide a home shopping service to the viewer for making responsive purchases by telephone or mail. The ancillary print or graphic information is "video multiplexed" on an unused or unseen portion of the main video signal. This information does not interfere with the normal reception of the main video signal, and the ancillary information can be "decoded out" and viewed simultaneously with or separately from the main TV program. The ancillary video information can be associated with or distinct from the main video program. The system is generally similar in concept to other subsidiary services like FM SCA, TV MTS, AM stereo, etc.— except that it is a video version thereof.

Historical Perspective.   Britain, France, and Canada each developed different versions of teletext systems in the late 1970s. Needless to say, American firms began to envision an American market, and began to support the U.S. adoption of one or another of these incompatible systems: Britain's Ceefax, France's Antiope, or Canada's Teledon. In 1979, CBS conducted teletext tests over its station in St. Louis, then expanded the testing to the Los Angeles market, and anticipates offering it to its affiliates on an advertiser-supported basis. NBC has indicated intentions of offering a service to its affiliates, and group broadcast owners have expressed interest and have begun experimentation. In 1981, the FCC initiated a Notice of Proposed Rulemaking to consider teletext as an authorized service, and additionally authorized a one-year experiment for a Chicago station to provide teletext service to 100 subscribers equipped with decoders. Educational TV stations also began experimenting. In March 1983, the FCC authorized the transmission of teletext by both full-service and low-power (LPTV) stations.

Regulatory Perspective.   The Commission authorized teletext service to be provided by television broadcast stations as a data system for the transmission of textual and graphic information intended for display on viewing screens. The FCC decided upon an "open" regulatory scheme to enhance the development of the service. No technical standards were established; broadcasters could employ whatever system suited their purposes, within the limits of not interfering with normal signals. The information distributed by teletext can be related to or distinct from the simultaneous main program. The service can be distributed to the public at large, to a limited audience, or to individual firms or persons. It can therefore be transmitted on a point-to-point or point-to-multipoint basis. Licensees are free to operate, franchise, or lease this service, which can be operated on an advertiser- or subscriber-supported basis. The FCC leaves it up to the licensee to determine whether his teletext service is broadcast, common carrier, or private communications; it will then be regulated under the appropriate rules.

Regulatory Problems.   As with most new technologies, teletext presents interesting problems. The FCC has declared it to be an ancillary service, not subject to broadcast regulations such as public service and equal access requirements. However, when used as a supplement to or enhancement of the broadcast program (such as captioning for the hearing impaired), that decision is called into question. The FCC's decree that the teletext portion of the TV signal is exempt from cable "must carry" rules is also questionable. If teletext is truly not subject to broadcast rules and is a "print" medium, there is cause to wonder at any regulation for it. The policy of the Commission permitting the licensee to determine the nature of his teletext service (as broadcast, common carrier, or private radio) for regulatory purposes has been undermined by recent court actions. Much remains to be resolved in teletext regulation.

Teletext Standards.   The FCC prescribed no technical standards for American teletext, other than that any teletext system must not interfere with the main channel of the station or with other station's signals. Broadcasters are permitted to employ any of the present, or future, competing systems. The three viable systems presently competing (which are incompatible with each other) are the British Ceefax, Canadian Teledon, and French Antiope. In light of the dilemma faced by the AM stereo industry, the retardation of the industry due to lack of a national standard, there is much reason to institute a standard—whether by decree or acclaim. AT&T and CBS are promoting a compromise standard called the North American Broadcast Teletext Specifications, which combines elements of the French and Canadian systems.

Teletext Defined.   The term *teletext* generally is applied to the system of multiplexing the video signal (as an ancillary information system) distributed by broadcast television stations, as opposed to cable or wire distribution. The teletext service, therefore, is necessarily a one-way, or noninteractive, service by which the ancillary video information is broadcast with a standard TV broadcast signal, and viewers equipped with a decoder can view the ancillary information. Viewers not so equipped merely see the main TV program. Viewers have no way to respond to the source of the information in this system—except perhaps by telephone.

Technological Overview.   At this point, the reader should be familiar with, or review, those sections of the book explaining the creation of the standard television video signal and multiplexing techniques. Teletext technology is a video version of multiplexing techniques discussed earlier. It is merely the process of utilizing unused portions or segments of the standard TV video signal to carry additional or ancillary video information. The ancillary video information is modulated upon video scan lines not used by the main TV picture, and subsequently separated therefrom by a special decoder to be viewed separately on the TV screen. The concept is very similar to FM SCA; the technology is video multiplexing.

Picture Conversion.   The television camera lens projects a pictorial image on the light-sensitive face of the camera pickup tube. Within the tube, an electron gun scans 525 times across the face of the tube, from left to right, starting from top to bottom. By this means, the gun converts the picture into 525 lines of electronic (video) signals, modulated with the light intensity variations detected within each line. Since the gun scans the entire face 30 times every second, one complete picture is produced every $\frac{1}{30}$ second; that is, 30 complete pictures every second are converted into an electronic signal representing the 525 lines of the picture in sequence. (Interlace scanning is irrelevant to this discussion.) This signal is displayed on the picture tube of the TV set by the reverse process. The electron gun in the picture tube scans the phosphorescent face of the tube in exact synchronization with the 525 lines of the incoming signal. The varying light intensities of each line are displayed on the face of the tube to reproduce the original complete picture. (Refer to the discussion of video in the section on broadcast television).

Video Blanking. In addition to the picture information, the video signal must carry to the TV set signals that will turn the picture tube gun off during the gun's retrace across the screen, so that the retraces are not visible. Thus, each line contains a pulse that turns off the picture tube gun during the period of retrace to start the next scan line. To turn off the picture tube gun during the longer retrace from bottom to top of the screen, or from the end of one picture to the start of the next, another pulse is included at the end of the 525th line. This pulse keeps the gun turned off for the time it takes to retrace from the bottom of one picture to the top of the next—the duration of 21 scan lines. Thus, the TV picture tube gun is turned off during the scanning of the first 21 lines of the video signal. The TV screen is designed so that the top 21 lines of video do not appear in the picture display area, and are not necessary to the picture. The video signal, therefore, contains 21 lines of unused space during what is called the *vertical blanking interval* (VBI). This space can be seen on the tube as a wide black line between pictures when the TV screen "rolls" due to improper vertical sync adjustment of the TV set (see Fig. 7-1).

Video Multiplexing. Since there are 21 unused lines within the video signal, these lines can be individually modulated by simple (print or graphic information) video not associated with the video of the main program (lines 22–525). It is merely a matter of electronically injecting this ancillary video information into the system during the period when the pickup tube gun is scanning one or more of these 21 lines—a video form of multiplexing. When the signal is received at the TV receiver, a normal TV set will not respond to this ancillary information, since the electron gun doesn't normally "see" this scan area. A TV set equipped with a decoder, however, can detect and extract the information on these lines for display on the picture tube.

Teletext Decoder. The subscriber's teletext decoder is a device that can distinguish the different lines within the TV scanning process. It can select one or more individual scan lines, store them temporarily in a built-in memory (like a microcomputer), and then display that line or those lines on the TV screen—simultaneously with or in the absence of the picture of the main video signal. An example of simultaneous display would be teletext service offering subtitling of programs for the hearing impaired, which would appear on screen across the bottom of the normal picture. Separate display would be switching the normal picture off and viewing only the selected line of information, which could

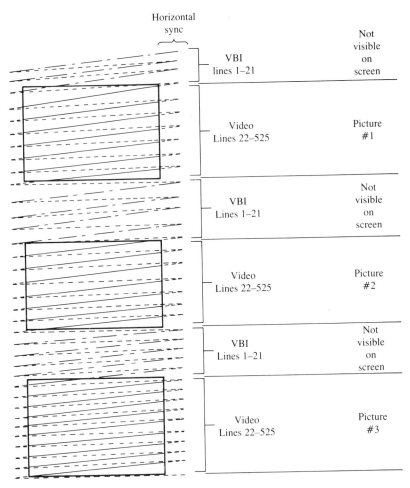

Figure 7-1 Normal TV signal scanning.

be displayed full screen. The decoder design provides the necessary capability for the system it is associated with (See Fig. 7-2).

Decoding Process. As the TV signal is being received normally, all 525 lines of video signal pass through the TV set as a single picture every 1/30 second, or 30 pictures per second. Any information on lines 1–21 will not be visible on a standard TV set, because these lines are not displayed in the picture. Sets equipped for teletext reception (normally a subscription service), however, will have an associated decoder and keypad. The keypad, similar to the keyboard of a hand calculator, can be operated by the viewer to select any of the 1–21 lines in the VBI. Normally, the decoder will then "grab" that particular line as it goes by, store it in a memory bank, turn the normal picture off the display, and display the information from the selected and stored line. This information will be displayed on the screen until a different line is selected or the teletext function is turned off and the TV set reverts to normal reception of the main picture.

Display Process.   The selected VBI line passes through the decoder every 1/30 second, and is stored in the memory. Each time the line passes through, it carries additional video information contributing to a complete picture, and is stored with the information delivered by the previous pass-through. Each time the selected line passes through the system, therefore, it adds additional information to a complete picture that is stored in the decoder's memory. As soon as the decoder has a single complete picture, it is displayed on the TV screen for as long as the viewer chooses to view it. The complete still picture is referred to as a *page* of text. The page being displayed is continually reinforced by the continuous repetition of the incoming line carrying the information, rebuilding the page over again and again for the memory, which repeatedly displays it as a composite picture.

An Example.   Assume that an entrepreneur has leased VBI line 10 of a local TV station to deliver to subscribers (equipped with leased decoders) for display on their TV sets a community calendar of events. She programs her computer with a complete video page of text. The computer sends this textual information by telephone line to the broadcast TV transmitter. During each VBI period of the transmission while line 10 is being broadcast, the computer modulates line 10 with the data representing a segment of the page of text. The next time line 10 is broadcast (1/30 second later), another segment of the page of text is modulated upon it. This continues until the complete page of text has been delivered by successions of line 10 being transmitted with each frame of the normal TV broadcast video. The viewers who select line 10 on their decoder will have the successive line 10s stored in their decoders' memory until the full page of text has been stored. The page will then be displayed on the TV screen as a full-screen page of information.

Updating Text.   As long as the computer keeps programming the same page to be repeatedly delivered by successive line 10s, the page is repeatedly memorized and repeatedly displayed. However, the computer can change or update information on this page of text, which will be delivered and reflected in the subsequent display. By this means, a page of text can be updated or changed continuously or repeatedly.

Multiple Pages.   The computer can be programmed with more than one page of text to be delivered. The computer merely feeds one page of text after another to the broadcast transmitter. The contents of page 1 will be delivered in segments by successive transmissions of the designated VBI line, and stored in the receiving terminal until completed for display. Then page 2 will be delivered by the same line repetitions, then page 3, etc. The time it takes to deliver a full page depends upon the complexity and amount of information in the text of each page. Therefore, a page containing simple alphanumeric (letters and numbers) information requires considerably less line repetitions than a page containing complex pictorial information. Thus, the simpler the page information, the faster it can be delivered; or conversely, the more complex the page, the longer period of time (repeated line transmissions) it requires to be delivered. The number of pages that can be delivered by a single VBI line is theoretically unlimited, one after another, ad infinitum. However, as the number and complexity of pages increases, the longer the viewer must wait for the selected picture to be delivered, stored, and available for display. Present technology permits about 100 to 200 pages of text to be delivered within what is considered an acceptable but arbitrary "wait time." The viewer's decoder is designed to be able to distinguish between pages, and he can therefore use the keypad to select not only a particular VBI line, but a specific page delivered by that line to be stored and displayed, while other pages delivered by the same line will be ignored.

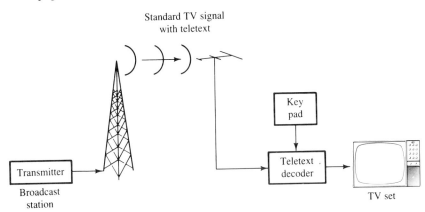

Figure 7-2 Teletext decoding.

VBI Multiple Lines. The Vertical Blanking Interval (VBI) consists of 21 lines. Lines 1–9 are used to provide vertical synchronization to the TV picture tube electron gun, so that it knows exactly when to start scanning each video frame or picture from the top of the screen down. (Each video line contains a pulse to synchronize the horizontal scanning of the gun.) Lines 10–13 are not presently used, but are dedicated for future teletext expansion. Lines 14–18 are presently authorized for teletext use [but lines 17 and 18 are shared with a vertical interval test function (VIT) of the TV signal]. Line 19 is reserved for a vertical interval reference signal (VIRS) to stabilize the color component of the regular TV main program video. Line 20 is shared by the teletext service and a programming source identification function of the station (SIDS). Line 21 has long been used for closed captioning for the hearing impaired, associated with the main channel TV program (see Fig. 7-3).

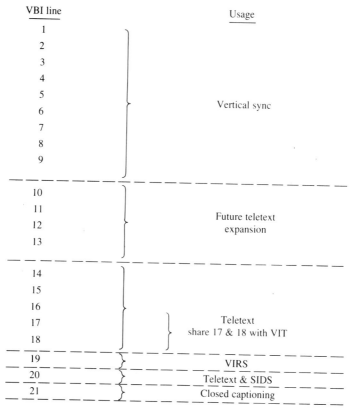

Figure 7-3   VBI utilization.

Closed-Caption Service.   Line 21 has traditionally been used to provide closed captioning text of the main program audio for the hearing impaired. This service has been largely developed and used by noncommercial TV stations, but some application of it exists in commercial television. This service provides that the sound portion of the TV program is translated into visual text. The visual text is multiplexed onto line 21 for delivery with the broadcast signal. Hearing-impaired persons are provided with a decoder that, when switched on, automatically detects line 21 and displays its text across the bottom of the screen simultaneously with the main program picture. This permits the hearing impaired to read the audio aspect of the program. Closed captioning cannot be seen on a standard screen without a decoder, which is different from "open captioning," which is delivered as part of the visual portion of the video signal and is visible on all TV screens.

Full Channel Teletext. The entire signal, or channel, of a TV broadcast station could technically be used to deliver teletext services instead of broadcast programming. If the station ceased normal broadcast programming to devote its channel exclusively to teletext services, it could use all of the 525 lines for teletext (except the few required for technical purposes). Each of these nearly 525 lines could be leased out to a different source for the delivery of their informational services. (The audio portion of the channel could even provide background music, could be leased to an audio service, or it too could carry data.) Viewers could be equipped with a keypad and decoder with which they could select any of the nearly 525 lines, and further select any page of the selected line for viewing. The total number of available pages would be truly awesome. Unfortunately, there is presently no advertiser or subscriber base adequate to make this concept economically viable, nor is it authorized by the FCC. It is, however, a future possibility—perhaps for the LPTV service. (This concept might also be viable for a cable TV channel, as discussed later under Videotex.)

Delivery Systems. Teletext is normally thought of as a service of the broadcast TV signal, specifically employing the VBI. The concept can as readily, however, be applied to any medium whose signal has an adequate bandwidth and an unused portion thereof. Ancillary video information of a still print or graphic nature (not involving constant motion or intricate detail) can technically be multiplexed into the signals of other services, such as FM radio, ITFS, OFS, MDS, telephone lines, and other media. With the accelerating developments in signal companding (compression-expansion techniques) technology, perhaps AM radio and other narrowband width radio services could soon employ simple teletext services. Presently, any medium that can carry the standard TV signal (with its VBI multiplexed) is a potential teletext delivery system: cable, translators, MDS, ITFS, CARS, satellites, and the like.

Summary. Teletext is a means of delivering print and graphic information ancillary to a standard television broadcast signal. A computer which stores pages of single frames of alphanumeric or pictorial information is connected to a standard TV broadcast transmitter. As the normal TV signal is transmitted, the computer causes a portion of a page of teletext information to be modulated upon unused scan lines within the vertical blanking interval (VBI) portion of the TV signal. This is repeated on the successive transmissions (every $\frac{1}{30}$ second) of the same unused lines until a complete page or pages of the text from the computer have been broadcast. The TV viewer subscribing to the teletext service is equipped with a decoder and keypad connected to the TV set. When the set is tuned to the TV channel carrying the teletext signal, the viewer can watch the main TV program or select to view instead any of the pages of teletext, which the decoder has detected and stored in its memory. Current technology permits over 100–200 pages of text to be delivered in this manner, but this capacity is expected to increase with technological advances. Teletext is a passive (view only) system, subject to regulation by the FCC.

VIDEOTEX

Overview.   Videotex serves essentially the same functions as does teletext, and for the same purposes, but its delivery system and capabilities differ. In other words, it is a somewhat different means to the same end. Videotex provides viewers with alphanumeric and pictorial (print and graphic) information, as does teletext, but it is delivered by wire or cable rather than by broadcast signals over conventional TV channels. Additionally, the term *videotex* is generally associated with wire/cable systems that provide interactive or two-way participation between source and individual viewer, but this is not always the case.

Historical Perspective.   Videotex and teletext are siblings, having been born in the same environment and era, of the same parentage of need and technology. The late 1970s saw their birth struggle, and the early 1980s have witnessed their infancy. Their common origins and purposes give them strong similarities; however, their divergent environments and potentials give them distinct differences. While the technical and regulatory restrictions of the broadcasting service curtail or limit the potential of teletext, videotex enjoys the generally unrestricted environment of wire and cable systems. This has permitted videotex to develop faster and further than teletext, and provides it with more vast horizons to pioneer in during its adolescence of the late 1980s.

Regulatory Perspective.   The technology of teletext is limited by the restrictions of the standards for broadcast television. Videotex does not suffer from this same limitation. As a creature of the wire and cable media, videotex enjoys relative freedom from regulation. When delivered by private wircline, it enjoys nearly total freedom from regulation. When delivered by telephone line, its regulation is the minimum imposed upon content regulation of common carriers. When carried by cable TV systems, its regulation is the minimum imposed to conform to the general technical specifications of cable systems to pass and prevent interference to broadcast signals carried on the cable. This relative freedom from regulation provides the developers of videotex with great latitude in design, experimentation, and application.

Delivery Systems. As indicated previously, videotex has normally two means of delivery, by wire [telephone (Telco) line] and by cable TV system. Of course, when a cable system carries a TV broadcast signal containing teletext, this is not considered videotex. Videotex is a service originated within the wire/cable system, whether by the system operator or by a marketing entrepreneur leasing the system (or a portion thereof) for the purpose. Private or Telco wireline systems are usually interactive (two-way). Cable system videotex provides a tremendous future for interactive videotex; however, present cable videotex is mostly passive (noninteractive), because most cable systems as yet are only one-way systems.

Cable VBI Videotex. A cable system operator can send videotex information down the system to subscribers in the identical manner of a broadcaster delivering teletext information to viewers. The cable operator can employ one of his local origination channels (such as a public access channel or automated news channel) to carry the videotex information. This technique employs a computer programmed with the videotex information to insert it on a selected line or lines of the vertical blanking interval (VBI) of the channel's normal TV signal during its origination at the system headend. The technique is identical to teletext. Cable subscribers who pay an additional subscription fee are supplied with keypad and decoder with which to view selected pages of videotex when tuned to the proper cable channel. This application is normally passive, in that the viewer can view the information, but not respond to it. Response can be made, however, by normal telephone to a telephone number indicated in the text on the TV screen.

Cable Full-Channel Simplex Videotex. The cable operator can use an entire channel for delivery of videotex to subscribers. This can be done in either of two ways. The simplest requires no keypad or decoders. It consists merely of the pages of videotex being sent down the channel, one at a time, using the entire signal to display a single page just as if a camera were viewing a page at a time at the headend. The viewer then merely tunes to the channel and observes the videotex pages in real time, or as they change by themselves on the screen. In this application, the viewer has no control over the pages, but can merely observe them as they change. Although this is a passive operation, the viewer could respond by telephone to references on any page of text. This application is arguably not videotex at all, since it involves no multiplexing process, but is merely alphanumeric automation.

Cable Full-Channel Multiplexed Videotex. Another full-channel videotex application does employ video multiplexing. As was described earlier as full-channel teletext for broadcast, the cable operator can multiplex each separate line (nearly 525 lines) of a full-channel video signal with multiple pages of videotex. The technique employed is precisely the same technique as for VBI teletext or VBI videotex, except that each line of the 525 (except those few dedicated to other uses) is used, instead of just those within the VBI. Remember that each line can theoretically deliver an unlimited number of pages; however, the more numerous and complex the pages, the longer is the wait time required for any single page to be delivered complete for the display. If all 525 lines of the channel are used for page delivery, however, a channel can theoretically deliver 525 times more pages than a single line (but 525 × infinite is unrealistic); or, more realistically, the channel can deliver pages 525 times faster. Thus, the effect of full channel multiplexed videotex is to increase tremendously the combination of page capacity, complexity of information, and speed of delivery over VBI videotex or teletext. The viewer would be required to subscribe to the videotex service, would be supplied with a keypad and decoder, could tune in the videotex channel and select innumerable subchannels (lines) of pages of text. Again, this application does not provide for interactive (responsive) capability other than by telephone.

Interactive Cable Videotex.   Truly interactive cable videotex requires a two-way cable system (see the section on cable TV technology). Any of the three configurations of two-way system (loop, upstream midband channels, or upstream shadow cable) would provide interactive capability. The viewer's keypad would have two functions built into it: page selection and response capability. Pressing coded buttons of the page selection function can select specific lines and pages of the incoming videotex channel for viewing. Pressing coded buttons of the response function will send coded digital signals out of the terminal on the paired upstream videotex channel to the headend. A response computer then senses and records the coded response (with its automatically coded residential address) for necessary action. This response function also can serve as an initiating action for access and retrieval of pages of text, providing a librarying function of the computer's stored pages of information. In this manner, subscribers can select and respond to information being distributed, or can command the computer to deliver specific pages of information (probably from a catalog) on demand, and can respond to it. This makes possible shopping, banking, responding to surveys, and doing many other activities from the home.

Cable Videotex Capacity Potential.   Broadcast teletext technology presently can provide a teletext service of about 100 to 200 pages of text. This same technology used for VBI videotex techniques permits approximately the same. However, full-channel multiplexed videotex using all lines of a TV channel (about 500 lines) theoretically provides this application with 500 times more page capacity. The potential exists for a different computer service representing a different agency to be available on each of the 500 video lines. It is conceivable that 50,000 pages of information could be available to subscribers on a single cable channel. (A demand access system can have an infinite page capacity, depending upon the computer storage.) The capacity and diversity potential for personal services is staggering.

Hard-Copy Printouts.   An additional capability that is presently "off the shelf" (available) technology is hard-copy printouts. For an additional lease-rent-sale fee, a videotex subscriber can be provided with a small printing unit similar to those that many home computers presently employ. This unit, connected to the TV set, can print out on a sheet of paper whatever text or graphic is visible on the TV screen, or is stored in the memory of the decoder. The viewer can then have a permanent copy of the information accessed or presented from the computer. Although defenders of copyright law shudder at the prospect, the reality of the availability and future demand for this service must be appreciated and contended with.

Public (Wireline) Videotex.   Another form of videotex that is springing up around the country is public videotex. This concept involves the delivery of videotex information from a computer to strategically located public terminals by wire, normally privately leased telephone line. These public terminals consist of a pay-telephone-type of booth containing a video screen with keypad panel. They are generally located in shopping malls, airports, tourist centers, and other places of heavy public pedestrian traffic. The technology employed is essentially the same as interactive (two-way) videotex on cable. The keypad can be used to access information from the computer on an upstream line, and then to select specific pages for viewing on the display screen as the information comes to the terminal on a downstream line. The number of pages the system can store and deliver is dependent upon the storage capacity of the computer and the frequency response bandwidth of the wireline (or coaxial cable). The capability for responses to the viewed information to be sent upstream to the computer can be included in the system. This system permits a member of the general public to stop at the terminal, access information (menus, catalogs, schedules, services, locations, etc.), and if desired, to respond with specific requests.

Public Videotex Potential.   This form of videotex, permitting a member of the general public to stop at the terminal, access specific information, and respond to that information with specific requests, opens up more avenues of public service. This capability provides a very convenient information source; however, the next logical extension is obviously of tremendous public service value in another way. If these terminals are equipped with a slot for credit cards, the viewer could view catalogs, menus, schedules, and other offerings, and additionally order and pay for merchandise, tickets, reservations, and the like. With hundreds of pages of text capability, a wireline videotex system becomes a viable and effective marketing tool for many individual and diverse service agencies and merchants simultaneously.

Public Videotex Activity.   In many cities, different variations and applications of public wireline videotex presently exist. Many banking institutions employ remote videotex terminals for patrons to do their banking from grocery stores, airports, and so on. Banking networks are in operation where several banks employ the same videotex system—banks, patrons, and accounts all being identified by the patron's inserting his plastic bank card and keying in his secret identification number. Additionally, in many cities systems have been established to provide shopping services, schedules of local entertainment and sports events, news, weather, directions for tourists, and many other services. Terminals have been placed in shopping malls, hotels, tourist and transportation centers, offices, and many other locations. The San Francisco Bay area is developing a system of 300 terminals to serve 11 counties, while Toronto is boasting a 900-page system of 400 terminals serving 200 sites. Other cities with public systems include Dallas, Orlando, Sacramento, Phoenix, Honolulu, Oklahoma City, and many others. About 30 companies are actively involved in public videotex system design, installation, and operation.

Personal Computer Videotex.   Another logical extension of videotex is to provide the service to home computers via cable TV systems or telephone line. Since many homes and offices are now equipped with home or personal computers, which are natural videotex terminals (consisting of memory, display, and keypad), a natural market exists for additional information services. The videotex entrepreneur need not provide the terminals (which are already owned by the subscribers), or provide the delivery system (the already existing telephone line or cable TV system). The entrepreneur need only provide a computer (information source) and lease a connection to the cable headend or telephone exchange. He can then market his services to both advertisers (information and service providers) and subscribing viewers (personal computer owners). Such home computer videotex systems are emerging, and their future growth is expected to rapidly accelerate and expand.

Summary.   Videotex is similar to teletext in purpose and technology. It is a means of delivering print and graphic information to viewers through a video multiplexing technique. As with teletext, videotex superimposes (or modulates) this digital information upon individual scan lines of a standard video signal. Videotex, however, employs cable or wireline as its delivery system rather than the broadcast signal. This permits videotex to use either the VBI of a TV channel, an entire empty channel of the cable, or the entire bandwidth of a telephone line to deliver the videotex information. In using an entire channel or wireline bandwidth, up to approximately 500 lines of video can be used instead of only the available lines within the 21-line VBI. Current technology can provide as many as 5000 pages of text on a cable channel, and an infinite number are possible. Additionally, cable or wireline systems can provide for interactive (two-way) capability, permitting viewers to respond to and access on demand the information in the computer. Since videotex employs cable or wireline, it is relatively free from FCC restrictions and regulations, which permits it great latitude and freedom in development and application.

selected bibliography

Federal Communications Commission Reports and Orders

FCC Docket No. 8736, 8975, 9175, 8976. Sixth Report and Order, adopted April 11, 1952. (Television assignments)

FCC Docket No. 21323. Second Report and Order, adopted March 29, 1984. (Authorization of TV audio subchannels—MTS)

FCC Docket No. 21502. Third Report and Order, adopted June 17, 1982. (Revision of subscription TV service—STV)

FCC Docket No. 78–253. Report and Order, adopted March 4, 1982. (Authorization for low-power TV—LPTV)

FCC Docket No. 80–112. Report and Order, adopted May 26, 1983. (Amendments to rules of ITFS, MDS, and OFS)

FCC Docket No. 80–603. Report and Order, adopted June 23, 1982. (Development of policy for DBS Service)

FCC Docket No. 81–741. Report and Order, adopted March 31, 1983. (Authorization of Teletext)

FCC Docket No. 82–536. First Report and Order, adopted April 7, 1983. (Amendment of SCA rules)

Federal Communications Commission Rules and Regulations, 1982

Title 47 Code of Federal Regulations (Available from the Superintendent of Documents, U.S. Government Printing Office, Washington, D.C., 20402.)

Part 2 Frequency Allocations and Radio Treaty Matters.

Part 5 Experimental Radio Services.

Part 15 Radio Frequency Devices.

Part 17 Construction, Marking, and Lighting of Antenna Structures.

Part 73 Radio Broadcast Services.

Part 74 Experimental, Auxiliary, and Special Broadcast and Other Program Distribution Services.

Part 76 Cable Television Service.

Part 78 Cable Television Relay Service.

Part 94 Private Operational-Fixed Microwave Service.

Part 100 Direct Broadcast Satellite Service.

Federal Communications Commission Pamphlets, Bulletins, and Reports

(Available from International Transcription Services, Inc., 4006 University Drive, Fairfax, VA, 22030.)

FCC Pamphlet #11, 3/78, *Frequency Allocation.*

FCC Pamphlet #16, 10/82, *Subscription Television.*

FCC Pamphlet #17, 7/79, *Public Radio.*

FCC Pamphlet #18, 8/83, *Cable Television.*

FCC OST Bulletin No. 60, April 1984, *Multichannel Television Sound Transmission and Audio Processing Requirements for the BTSC System.*

FCC OPP Staff Report, September 1980, *Policies for Regulation of Direct Broadcast Satellites.*

National Association of Broadcasters Publications

(Available from The National Association of Broadcasters, 1771 N St. NW, Washington, D.C. 20036.)

Broadcast Engineering Conference Technical Papers, 1983.

Broadcasting and Government, 1984.

Broadcasting Bibliography, 1982.

Business Opportunities for Broadcasters in MDS Pay Television, 1982.

Buying or Building a Broadcast Station, 1982.

Communications Satellites: Overview and Options for Broadcasters, 1982.

Direct Broadcast Satellite Study, 1981.

Direct Broadcast Satellites: Service, Economic and Market Factors, 1981.

NAB Engineering Handbook, 1975.

New Technologies Affecting Radio and Television Broadcasting, 1982.

New Technologies: Bridging the Distance to a New Communications Age, 1983.

Radio, New Technology and You, 1982.
Radio Subcarrier Services, 1983.
Radio Today—and Tomorrow, 1982.
SMATV: Strategy Opportunities in Private Cable, 1982.
Subscription Television: History, Current Status, and Economic Projections, 1980.

Periodical Articles

"The New Order Passeth: A Long, Hard Look at Promise Versus Performance of the New Media," *Broadcasting,* December 10, 1984, p. 43.

"Special Report: After 10 Years of Satellites, The Sky's No Limit," *Broadcasting,* April 9, 1984, p. 43.

"Sorting Out the DBS Proposals," *Broadcasting,* January 16, 1984, p. 48.

JOE DEANGELO, "AM Stereo: Soon on the Air?" *Popular Electronics,* December, 1978, p. 59.

PETER UTZ, "How Cable TV Works," *AV Video,* May, 1984.

CARL BENTZ, "LPTV Notes: An Industry Begins to Expand," *Broadcast Engineering,* March, 1984, p. 88.

JACQUELYN BIEL AND JOHN KAMPOS, "LPTV Success Stories," *Videopro,* March, 1984, p. 18.

LEONARD FELDMAN, "TV Stereo: A System Closeup," *BM/E (Broadcast Management and Engineering),* March, 1984, p. 119.

JOHN KINIK, "Satellite Update," *Broadcast Engineering,* January, 1984, p. 12.

DELBERT D. SMITH AND MARTIN A. ROTHBLATT, "Geostationary Platforms: Legal Estates in Space," *Journal of Space Law,* Vol. 10, No. 1 (Spring 1982), The University of Mississippi.

JILL ABESHOUSE STERN, ERWIN G. KRASNOW, AND R. MICHAEL SENKOWSKI, "The New Video Marketplace and The Search for a Coherent Regulatory Philosophy," *The Catholic University Law Review,* Vol. 32, No. 3 (Spring 1983).

Doctoral Dissertations

GEORGE E. WHITEHOUSE, "A Conceptual Model for the Utilization of Community Cable Television for Institutional-Community Educational Service," The University of Southern Mississippi, 1974.

index